The Busy Family's Guide to Volunteering

Acknowledgments

There are no words to describe the work and dedication that Marla Kinney has put into this book and into all my writing. She's both enormously talented and unfailingly generous. I have no idea what I would do without her.

My so-kind editors at Robins Lane Press, Kate Kuhn and Kathy Charner, have provided creative ideas, patience, and enthusiasm. Their belief in this book has turned my dream into reality. I'm forever grateful.

A special thanks to the parents and children who shared their stories. Although not all of them have made it into these pages, each of them lives the belief that caring for one another heals the world. We're all blessed that they give so much.

Many thanks to all those who read, listened, made thoughtful suggestions, and convinced me that I had something to contribute, especially Joe Chrastil, Anne Damon, Scott Edelstein, Laura Friedman, Linda Klein, Tim Klein, Mary Purnell, Sarah Steefel, Gretchen Thompson, Kathy Watson, and Mike Young.

Most of all, my thanks and forever love to Rocky, my husband and dear friend, and my children, Jessie, Rachel, and Nick. They've supported me every step of the way and have always, always believed in me. How could I have gotten so lucky?

Dedication

To the memory of Paul and Sheila Wellstone, who fought so hard for what I believe in. We all miss you more than we can say.

And for Jessie, Rachel, Nick, Carolyn, Becky, Sarah, Kim, Nathan, Mitch, and all children everywhere. Carry it forward.

The Busy Family's Guide to Volunteering

Do good, have fun, make a difference as a family!

JENNY FRIEDMAN

Robins Lane Press
A division of Gryphon house, Inc.
Beltsville, Maryland

Copyright © 2003 Jenny Friedman
Published by Robins Lane Press
10726 Tucker Street, Beltsville, MD 20705
800-638-0928 * 301-595-9500 * 301-595-0051 (fax)
Visit us on the web at www.robinslanepress.com

Library of Congress Cataloging-in-Publication Data

Friedman, Jenny Lynn, 1955-
  The busy family's guide to volunteering / by Jenny Friedman.
      p. cm.
Includes index.
  ISBN 1-58904-012-0
  1. Voluntarism--United States. 2. Family--United States. 3.
Family--Time management. I. Title.
  HN90.V64F75 2003
  302'.14--dc21

                                                          2003012054

Bulk purchase

Robins Lane Press books are available for special premium and sales promotions as well as for fund-raising use. Special editions or book excerpts also can be created to specification. For details, contact the Director of Marketing at the address above.

Disclaimer

The publisher and the author cannot be held responsible for injury, mishap, or damages incurred during the use of or because of the information in this book. Appropriate and reasonable caution and supervision of young children is recommended at all times. Every effort has been made to locate copyright and permission information. All information has been deemed accurate at press time, but may be subject to change.

Printed in the United States of America
10   9   8   7   6   5   4   3   2   1

Table of Contents

Introduction

Caring and compassion are two of the most important values parents hope to instill in their children. We want our kids to learn responsibility to their communities and we want to provide them with the tools they need to make a difference. And certainly each of us wants to do our part to build a better world. But how can we inspire the spirit of service in our children while also contributing to the greater good ourselves? Family volunteering can be one powerful answer.

You may not think a small family can do much to heal a troubled world. Our planet faces enormous challenges of poverty, injustice, and environmental degradation. Our children are often bombarded with messages promoting materialism, consumption, and entitlement. Yet each time we volunteer, we have an opportunity to teach our children that every human being has worth, that we are stewards of this planet, that the world is a better place when we care for others and they care for us. Finding the time to volunteer can be an obstacle for any family. But as it turns out, lessons can be taught, people's lives changed, and small miracles wrought in only minutes or hours. In fact, you'll find that contributing to the community can be woven into the fabric of everyday life with surprisingly little effort.

Most people think of volunteering as donating canned goods to a local food pantry or collecting mittens for low-income children during the holidays. And indeed those are excellent examples of doing for others. But in this book, "volunteering" is much more. It includes a whole range of ways we can give back to the community: serving a meal at a homeless shelter or bringing brownies to a new neighbor; walking dogs at the humane society or taking part in an anti-fur rally; tutoring in your local school or in a remote village in Mexico. The volunteer project your family chooses may last a few minutes or a few years. It may involve service work, social action, political engagement, or environmental activism. But in every case, you'll be doing something to improve the planet while passing on the values of integrity, kindness, and good stewardship.

It's important to remember that whatever you do, whether it's a short-term commitment or a lengthy project, an act of social justice or social service, it should always be positive and enjoyable for your family. And that means banishing the guilt. Rather than focusing on the things you aren't doing or admonishing yourself for failing to take on even more, acknowledge how much you already contribute, both to your family and to your community. Whenever you decide on a volunteer project—whether it's a walk to raise money for your favorite charity or an hour at your local park picking up litter—reflect on the positive difference you're making. When searching for new opportunities, continue to focus on those activities that will bring pleasure to both you and your kids.

Children of any age can contribute. When my daughter was an infant, she came along while a friend of mine and our two preschoolers delivered meals to the homebound. My son began cooking with us at a homeless shelter when he was just a toddler. Both children brought joy to the people we served simply by being present. Certainly family volunteering may be more work at first than volunteering single-handedly. (An older child had to supervise my two-year-old while we cooked, for example.) But having your kids with you makes volunteering more fun, and it's a wonderful way to share time together. Besides, those little ones can turn into extraordinarily helpful workers later on as community service becomes an integral part of their lives.

If you would like more information about how to engage with your children in community service, charitable giving, or social, political and environmental action, or if you would be willing to share your ideas or stories, visit the nonprofit organization Doing Good Together at www.doinggoodtogether.org.

How Can Busy Families Volunteer? 1

For busy parents who want to spend time with their children while still contributing to their communities, family volunteering is an opportunity to combine two commitments into one. All over the country, families cook at shelters, befriend international visitors, work with the elderly, help with environmental projects, and engage in countless other volunteer efforts. The rewards for these families are important lessons in compassion, empathy, and community responsibility. In addition, family volunteering can be an extraordinary educational tool. Depending on the volunteer job, children can gain knowledge of other cultures and languages, money matters, environmental issues, or the political process. But the benefits of volunteering as a family extend beyond the moral and academic lessons it provides. Many families feel that it brings them closer together by improving communication and enriching their relationships.

Something for Everyone

"Family" can mean anything from two parents and several children to a grandparent and grandchild, a noncustodial parent and his or her children, a foster parent and child, or a father and daughter duo. (Families also can consist of adults only; however, this book focuses specifically on families with children between infancy and adolescence.) And families of all configurations and income levels can make volunteering a part of their lives. One family rakes leaves for their elderly neighbors. Two gay men and their child work together to support other families with same-sex parents. A single mom and her two sons serve dinner at a homeless shelter for men. And a three-generation family works together to provide meals to the homebound each week.

Sometimes families have a stake in their volunteer activities, such as a family who decided to participate in a fundraising walk each year after their child was diagnosed with juvenile diabetes. Other families find out about opportunities through their churches, temples or synagogues, Girl or Boy Scout troops, or 4-H clubs. In these cases, parents often accompany a group of young people (including their children) to repair homes in low-income areas, collect teddy bears to comfort children in ambulances, or pick up litter along a highway. Sometimes it is the child's passion that serves as the motivator. One preteen who desperately wanted to spend time with animals convinced her mother and a friend to walk dogs and play with kittens at a local animal shelter.

Every family has something to contribute. And every family, at some time or another, benefits from and depends on the services of other volunteers. One family may coordinate a food drive for the hungry, but that same family may

WHO ARE FAMILY VOLUNTEERS?

According to the 2001 Independent Sector report *America's Family Volunteers*:

- ☼ 51% of all volunteers had taken part in some volunteer activity with a family member.
- ☼ The larger the household size, the more often families volunteered together.
- ☼ *Family volunteers averaged 4.3 hours of volunteering each week (compared to 2.8 hours for those who did not volunteer with family members).
- ☼ 35% of family volunteers worked in education, while 30% volunteered in human services.
- ☼ 45% of family volunteers did so regularly (compared to 33% of other volunteers).
- ☼ 90.6% of family volunteers said compassion for those in need was one reason they volunteered.
- ☼ One-third of family volunteers learned about their volunteer activity through a religious organization.
- ☼ 37% had a family member or friend who benefited from the activity.
- ☼ 52% of family volunteers were female, and 48% were male (59% of non-family volunteers were female).
- ☼ 53% of family volunteers had children under 18 living at home.

volunteering

profit from people volunteering to raise money for Alzheimer's disease, maintaining trails in our parks, or working to reduce global warming. All of us are givers and receivers, contributing what we can and benefiting from the bounty of what we obtain from others.

It is critical that we help our children understand this cooperative nature of community service, encouraging them to value and respect those who benefit from their family's volunteer efforts, and also to appreciate those individuals and families who have improved their life through kindness and service. If children don't comprehend this balanced ethic of service, they may, despite good intentions, take a patronizing attitude toward the elderly people in the nursing home you visit or the homeless men in the shelter where your family serves a meal. "There is an ongoing struggle to help young people see that they have something to offer, but to do that in ways that are not demeaning or condescending to those they serve," says Eugene Roehlkepartain, co-author of *Growing Up Generous: Engaging Youth in Giving and Serving* (Roehlkepartain et al, 2000). One way to accomplish this is to build relationships with those individuals your family serves.

Spend time getting to understand their lifestyle and culture and allow them to guide you in what kinds of help are most needed.

Also, reflect with your children on the help you provide, discussing together how it can be offered in a respectful manner. Talk about those occasions when you've depended on the goodwill of others and how it has enriched your lives.

Despite its benefits, many families feel that they're simply too busy to make the commitment to community service. But family volunteering does not need to involve hours each week or continue for weeks each year. You and your daughter may decide to spend one spring morning each year working at a local arts fair and then have a picnic lunch together. Or your family could make registering voters an annual family tradition. You'll discover that a long-term commitment is not necessary to reap the rewards of volunteering. This book is full of simple, one-time volunteer opportunities for busy families, as well as more long-term activities for those who are interested. In addition, what initially may seem like another task to check off the to-do list can actually be a time of renewal. If spending time with your children is something you value, then family volunteering will work for you.

The Benefits of Family Volunteering

Of all the activities you and your family do together in a lifetime, few will return the same rewards as spending time in community service work together. Families who volunteer note that volunteering teaches important values: compassion, empathy, gratitude, good stewardship, and community responsibility. With family volunteering, you can share your values with your children through example, rather than simply paying lip service to them. In addition, when children see kids in a homeless shelter or families coping with chronic illnesses or disabilities, it increases their appreciation for what they have.

Likewise, when they've spent time helping prepare a soup supper at the local community center or taken part in the annual town parade they feel the value of the community and they want to take care of it. In a culture that so often appears to reward materialism and greed, volunteering is an ideal way to live the meaning of loving-kindness. "My children learned more in their weeks of volunteering than I could teach in 10 years of Sunday school," says a parent of three young children.

Working together helps kids feel valued, acquire new skills, learn about life, and gain a more realistic view of the workplace. In our society, children seldom have the opportunity to contribute in a significant way to the well-being of the community. However, with volunteering, they know they're making a real difference in people's lives. One parent says that some of her friends were surprised to learn that her children were spending all day, every day for two weeks at an agency established to help local people cope with a devastating fire. But her children happily turned down invitations to the local swimming pool to spend their time helping others. Diane Wilson, of University Park, Texas, who went with her 17-year-old son, Chris, and other church members to lay a floor for a small church in Costa Rica, agrees. "Volunteering makes kids feel valuable and that they're being truly useful." Children who volunteer become aware of their talents and abilities, and that builds self-esteem, a sense of accomplishment, and confidence. And, in some cases, the skills they acquire may lead them to a career or life interest.

Family volunteering leads children to a new appreciation of other family members, sparks meaningful conversations, and builds stronger family bonds. Spending time together in significant work can prompt discussions about values and feelings and improve communication among family members. One family with children between the ages of 5 and 13 has been responsible for the same meals-on-wheels route for six years. One of the stops is an older woman with emphysema who continues to smoke. Getting to know this woman and watching her become increasingly ill and struggle for each breath has sparked a lot of discussions in the family about the health risks of smoking. "I don't think my kids would touch a cigarette," says this Memphis parent.

Other families have had important conversations about protecting the environment, aging, premarital sex, and financial responsibility. Paul Erlbaum and Rachael Grossman of East Montpelier, Vermont, saw a change in their family dynamics after a two-week

LEARNING TOLERANCE

Volunteering breaks down stereotypes and teaches tolerance. When volunteering with individuals of different ages, incomes, nationalities, and lifestyles, families gain a new understanding of the world community. They also learn to accept people's differences and appreciate people's struggles. On 11-year-old Benny Witkovsky's first visit with his mother to cook a meal at a homeless shelter for men in Madison, Wisconsin, he found something altogether different than what he expected. The grizzled and grumpy stereotype of homeless people he'd garnered from movies and television was replaced by the men he met that evening—"regular guys" with interests and moods and families and stories to tell. "They were nice. We talked to them. One guy had a kid in Appleton. Another guy had come up from Texas. A lot of them had jobs; they just didn't have enough money to get a place to stay," says Benny.

Through volunteering, some families get their first chance to spend time with people with disabilities, people from other countries or cultures, or people with different religions and lifestyles. This is an ideal opportunity to begin a conversation with your children about people's differences. But keep in mind that gaining awareness and sensitivity to diversity is a lifelong process. The most important thing is learning to respect (and helping your children learn to respect) what you may not always understand. Here are some ways to encourage your child to celebrate human differences.

1. Examine your own culture and cultural biases with your children. Let them know how many things are influenced by culturally based values and beliefs, including how we raise our children, how close we stand to other people, what kind of art we prefer, and how we celebrate and grieve. Confess to your child when you make a biased comment or treat some people less than fairly, and let them know that you're also working on learning tolerance and understanding. (To take a test to reveal any hidden biases, go to www.tolerance.org.)

2. Learn about the particular culture, disability, or religion of the people you and your family are getting to know through volunteering. Encourage those you're with to talk about themselves and their lives.

(continued on the next page)

stint volunteering together on an organic farm in Mogliazze, Italy, with their daughter, Leah, 17, and son, Ari, 11. "Our family has always worked well together," says Erlbaum. "But on our trip our relationship became more of a partnership. Now our children have more reasons than ever to be team players." Another Vermont parent who worked regularly on political campaigns and social action causes with her now-grown son, had a similar experience: "It built something much deeper between us than the usual parent-child bond."

Volunteering can lead to knowledge in a variety of areas. It is generally accepted that people learn best through hands-on experiences, so what better way to gain skills than by working as a volunteer? Working on a project to save the rainforest can teach children about biodiversity and ecology. Volunteering on a political campaign can help kids understand the workings of American democracy more powerfully than any high school civics class. And taking vacation

3. If someone who is not a native English speaker has trouble understanding you, try slowing down your speech (but use normal volume), using nonverbal cues (pointing, gestures, pictures), using simple present tense, and avoiding slang.

4. Be sure to give your children messages that contradict stereotypes. Begin these "anti-bias" lessons early. Read children's books with characters from other cultures and talk to your kids about what they see. Read about children with disabilities and successful adults with disabilities. Watch television with your child and point out the stereotypes you observe. Go to ethnic festivals in your community. Introduce your child to friends who represent a variety of lifestyles, cultures, and religions.

5. Keep the lines of communication open. Answer your children's questions and respond to their comments about differences they observe. Intervene if you ever hear your child make remarks that are racist, homophobic, sexist, or mean. Don't get angry, but don't let your child make the excuse that he or she was "just kidding" either. Explain why the comments bothered you and how they might be hurtful to others.

6. Make your home reflect cultural diversity by the art, music, and books you display; the movies and television shows you choose to watch; and the restaurants your family frequents.

volunteering

time to repair homes in Ecuador is certain to provide a new perspective on other cultures and improve everyone's Spanish-speaking skills.

Volunteering makes people happier and healthier. In a study of older adults (2,754 adults over a period of 9 to 12 years), Dr. James House of the University of Michigan Research Center discovered that volunteering, more than any other activity, increased life expectancy. But older people aren't the only ones who benefit. A 1995 Search Institute study found that youth who volunteer, even just one hour a week, are less likely to abuse drugs, alcohol, and cigarettes. "If you fill up a vacuum with something good," said one mother who volunteers with her four children, "something bad won't fall in there." In addition, youth who volunteer are more likely to do well in school, graduate, vote, and be philanthropic. For all of us, it seems, volunteering aids health and well-being.

Children who volunteer are more likely to become volunteering adults. According to a 2002 Independent Sector report, "Engaging Youth in Lifelong Service," adults who volunteered as children were two times more likely to be involved in community service as adults who didn't. These individuals learned the value of volunteering at an early age and are likely to continue contributing to the community throughout their lives.

Volunteering is fun, and apparently that's especially true when people volunteer with family members. Another survey by the Independent Sector found that while volunteers without family members gave an average of 2.8 hours per week, those who volunteered with their families gave 4.3 hours per week (from the 2001 Independent Sector Report, "America's Family Volunteers" based on results from the 1999 *Giving and Volunteering in the United States* survey). The enjoyment you'll find when you take the time to serve others is the most important reason of all to make family volunteering a part of your lives.

Growing Kids Who Care

Many parents have one goal in common when contemplating family volunteering: They want to raise caring, compassionate kids. But this is not always a given. Children's differences in "caring behavior" are due in part to inborn temperamental differences. Some kids are simply more sociable and optimistic and less fearful than others. However, researchers have identified specific child-rearing practices that encourage the development of kind, caring behavior. Dr. Ervin Staub, professor of psychology at the University of Massachusetts and author of *A Brighter Future: Raising Caring and Nonviolent Children* (in press), suggests ways parents can encourage compassion:

☼ Build a foundation of love and affection. From the first day, babies need responsive, predictable care from a loving caregiver. That means when your baby cries, pick her up and comfort her. Later, let your kids know you understand what they're feeling, allow them to express their opinions and emotions, share activities, and praise good behavior. Children need to have their own emotional needs satisfied before they can reach out to others.

☼ Point out the consequences of your child's unkind behavior. Even if your child's actions are unintentional, it's important to explain how his or her hurtful behavior affected the injured party. ("It hurts Karen and makes her sad when you grab her doll. How would you feel if someone took your favorite toy?") This goes beyond simply explaining that the behavior is wrong, but also providing an understanding of how the other person might be feeling. The tone in which you convey this information is important. Parents who are most effective are those who generally speak lovingly to their kids but use a serious and firm voice when describing the consequences of their child's unkindness.

☼ Also point out the consequences of your child's kind behavior. Make this a part of your family's discussions of any community service projects. For example, when you and your children make greeting cards to pass out at a veterans' hospital, explain how receiving a card and a visit makes the patients feel cared for and assuages their loneliness. Let your children know how proud you are of any good deeds and describe just how their actions make a difference in other people's lives.

☼ Expand caring beyond your immediate circle. You can pass on the message of tolerance by including all types of people—of different religions, ethnic groups, and lifestyles—in your circle of friends and acquaintances. And, whenever possible, have your children participate in activities that include a diverse group of kids.

☼ Have your child practice caring. Arrange opportunities for your child to do good deeds. Reaching out to others through volunteering or other acts of kindness not only makes children mindful of other people's needs, but also makes them aware of their own power to make a difference.

☼ Model caring. Let your child see you reaching out to others. Hold the door for a woman pushing a stroller or allow another driver into a heavy line of traffic. Tell your children about your own volunteer work and explain why you're taking food to a neighbor who's ill. The more you exhibit the values of kindness and generosity, the more you'll nourish them in your children.

10 Common Hesitations You May Have

Certainly, you can find plenty of good reasons for your family to become volunteers. But that doesn't mean it's easy to get started. In fact, it can be a little frightening. What are your concerns? Are you anxious about the lack of time? Uneasy about your child's emotional well-being? Here are the most common worries parents may have about volunteering with their kids, along with some solutions.

1. **My children are too young for volunteering.** It's true. Many volunteer jobs are simply inappropriate for younger children. Taking your baby to tutor in an elementary school would be disruptive. And a preschooler would get restless and bored if he needed to stuff envelopes for an hour. (Hardly a positive family experience!) But some jobs are suitable for younger children—even infants—such as visits to nursing homes, charity walks, litter clean-up, and others. (See "Developmental Timetable for Child Volunteers" in the Appendix.) As your children grow, you can find new opportunities to fit their evolving ages, interests, and schedules.

2. **I'm worried about having my children become depressed or frightened by what they see when volunteering.** When making a decision about family volunteering, it is important to consider your children's ages and temperaments. Certain children, at certain ages, may not be comfortable working in a hospital or even a homeless shelter. But most volunteer jobs are anything but depressing. For example, organizing a fundraiser or a recycling drive isn't frightening, it's energizing. Keep in mind that exposure to a variety of lifestyles and life issues is critical if we want our children to grow into compassionate people. What's important is how you help them integrate the experience. Use family volunteering as an opportunity to express your values and share your sense of responsibility to the community.

3. **Our family is already overbooked. We simply don't have time to volunteer.** Time is in short supply for every family. And it's important to be realistic about what you can take on. But the time crunch is actually a good reason to volunteer together. We all want to spend more time with our children, but sports, school activities, and work can get in the way. Family volunteering is a fun, low-cost, and meaningful way to be together. It's an opportunity for your family to enjoy one another after spending time on individual pursuits. It can involve a brief, one-time effort (just pick up an extra canned good at the grocery store for later delivery to a food shelf) or a long-term commitment (delivering meals once a month to the homebound).

4. **We can't take on a long-term commitment.** That's fine! As you'll see, this book is filled with hundreds of one-time (or "episodic") volunteer opportunities (also check out "Easy, Same-Day, No-Planning Family Volunteer Projects" in the Appendix). You might want to set aside National Family Volunteer Day (see page 29) for community service or volunteer together on Thanksgiving or Easter. Families can also volunteer once or twice a year for special events or projects.

5. **I would love for us to volunteer together, but my kids aren't interested.** It's important that children not feel forced or coerced into volunteering or performing

acts of kindness. But almost all kids can become enthusiastic about volunteering if it's the right activity at the right time. Here are tips for getting your kids excited about community service.

- Get them involved in choosing the activity and the time. (And be mindful that weekend dates or Saturday morning cartoons may be sacred.) When children feel they have a choice about what you'll be doing and that they contributed to the decision, they're more likely to be engaged.

- Invite their friends to join the volunteer effort. Especially as children get closer to the teenage years, everything is more fun when peers are included. Or, if you'd prefer, get another family involved that has children the same ages as yours.

- Choose an opportunity that fits their interests and personalities. Don't choose a sedentary activity for an active kid or a social opportunity for a child who is shy.

- Make the day fun. When I used to deliver meals with my kids, we'd always have a picnic afterwards and play on a playground.

- Appeal to their conscience. Let them know how important it is to help make the world a better place, and how significant their contribution can be.

- Pick an activity in which the child is recognized for his or her efforts. One family who volunteers at a nursing home is invited each year to a recognition ceremony. They receive prizes and lots of attention. What kids wouldn't be delighted about that?

- Show excitement about what you're doing. And make sure that when you begin volunteering, you keep it fun and light.

6. **We tried to volunteer together before, but it didn't work out.** That can happen, but don't give up. Sometimes the job simply doesn't match the family. Try again and this time be certain to fit the activity to your personality and interests. Or do something that makes a difference for someone you care about (such as fundraiser for leukemia research if you know a child suffering from the disease) or that has tangible rewards.

7. **Between sports and school activities, it's rare that everyone is available at the same time.** What if one time each month everyone put aside what they were doing to spend time together volunteering? Find a time when there are less likely to be conflicts—a Sunday evening or Saturday morning, perhaps. Then make it a priority. If that doesn't work, have your family break into smaller groupings. A father and daughter might volunteer together, and other times mother and son, or choose an activity that family members can participate in whenever they are available. Everyone doesn't have to participate each time you volunteer.

8. **The places I've contacted aren't interested in family volunteers.** Many agencies have never used family volunteers and may be uncertain how it will work. Emphasize that you will be responsible for supervising the children, and explain that your family has something significant to contribute: "My family would like to volunteer. Here are some things that we can do," or "Here are some ways I think that my first grader could be engaged in your agency." This approach is particularly helpful for organizations that may not have been forced to think outside the traditional volunteer box. If you'd like to find nonprofits in your area that are specifically requesting family volunteers, call your local volunteer center or 1-800-VOLUNTEER.

9. **My children are widely different ages.** Many jobs that are appropriate for younger children can be equally engaging for older ones (see "Developmental Timetable for Child Volunteers" in the Appendix) because each member of the family takes on different responsibilities. One example is serving a meal at a shelter or soup kitchen. Older children can help with the food preparation; younger ones can set the table. You might also consider visiting a nursing home, delivering meals, working on a social action project, or organizing a fundraiser. In each of these cases, there are a variety of jobs and everyone can contribute.

10. **I don't have time to organize volunteer activities for my family.** Consider ways to make the planning process less time-consuming. Choose an activity that doesn't require any advance sign-up. Your family might simply reserve a Saturday morning to clean up a local park, shop for items and deliver them to a local food shelf, or write a letter to the editor on an issue that concerns you (see "Easy, Same-Day, No-Planning Volunteer Activities" in the Appendix). Another way to find get organized is to contact a City Cares organization in your area (visit www.citycares.org to find out if there's one near you) and let them do the legwork for you. This group organizes the volunteer activities; you can select those that seem appropriate for your family. Or check out the social action or service committee at your church, temple, or synagogue to see what volunteer projects are available. Finally, visit www.familycares.org and pick out a project.

One working mother of three children between the ages of 4 and 13 describes the appeal of family volunteering:

> *I wanted to do volunteering personally and I kept having to say no to people because I felt like every time I said yes to a volunteer job I was taking time away from my family and it felt wrong to me. What I started to do was just send checks to everybody and I thought, At this point in my life I'll write checks, and then in the next part of my life, when my kids grow up, I'll give time. But that didn't feel right either. I felt like I really wanted to be doing something. So the idea of family volunteering seemed so perfect. Then I could do what I wanted to do, plus teach my kids about the value of service.*

volunteering

THE HOMESCHOOLED FAMILY

Both volunteering and homeschooling have been part of the life of Emily Wilson, 15, of Charlottesville, Virginia and her brothers Luke, 14, and Daniel, 13, since they were small. The kids, along with parents Mary and Jack, have delivered meals to the homebound, produced and distributed the neighborhood newsletter, cleaned up the neighborhood park and highway, built trails, and hosted mentally disabled adults in their home. As a result, the kids have become civic-minded themselves and each child now sees volunteering as an opportunity to explore his or her own interests and passions.

Emily, a budding social scientist, assists a researcher at a University of Virginia psychology laboratory. Daniel, a gifted mechanic, helps out at a local bike shop. And Luke had the confidence to stand in front of the city council in support of a plan to put up a large chalkboard in the downtown mall for citizens to express themselves.

There are, in fact, all kinds of benefits of family volunteering for homeschooled children. Volunteer jobs are often more interesting and more educational than paid employment, so children can gain important skills. And homeschooled families are available for volunteering during hours when most other families have children in school, which means greater flexibility in finding an opportunity that's right for every family member. Homeschooled children who volunteer not only learn their academic lessons in a "hands-on" way, but often form relationships with adults who may serve as mentors and teachers. And, says Mary, when her children have volunteered—both with the family and on their own—they've received glowing letters of recommendation from the agencies they serve: "Each of my children has a terrific resume as a result of volunteering," she says.

Resources

Books for Kids

Chicken Soup for Little Souls: The Goodness Gorillas by Lisa McCourt (Deerfield Beach, Florida: Health Communications, Inc., 1997). Ages 4-7.

The Giving Tree by Shel Silverstein (New York: HarperCollins Juvenile Books, 1987). Ages 4-8.

Kids' Random Acts of Kindness by Dawna Markova (Berkeley, CA: Conari Press, 1994). Ages 4-8.

The Legend of the Bluebonnet by Tomie de Paola (New York: Putnam Publishing Group, 1996). Ages 4-8.

The Rainbow Fish by Marcus Pfister, translated by J. Alison James (New York: North South Books, 1992). Ages 4-8.

Swimmy by Leo Lionni (New York: Knopf, 1992). Ages 4-8.

A Kid's Guide to Service Projects: Over 500 Service Ideas for Young People Who Want to Make a Difference by Barbara Lewis (Minneapolis: Free Spirit Publishing, 1995). Ages 9-12.

Kindness: A Treasury of Buddhist Wisdom for Children and Parents by Sarah Conover (Spokane, WA: Eastern Washington University Press, 2001). Ages 9 and up.

Catch the Spirit: Teen Volunteers Tell How They Made a Difference by Susan K. Perry (New York: Scholastic Library Publishing, 2000). Young adult.

A Complete Idiot's Guide to Volunteering for Teens by Preston Gralla (New York: Penguin Group, 2001). Young adult.

It's Our World, Too!: Stories of Young People Who Are Making a Difference by Phillip Hoose (New York: Farrar, Straus, and Giroux, 2002). Young adult.

Teens with the Courage to Give: Young People Who Triumphed over Tragedy and Volunteered to Make a Difference by Jackie Waldman (Berkeley, CA: Conari Press, 2000). Young adult.

Books for Parents

Chicken Soup for the Volunteer's Soul: Stories to Celebrate the Spirit of Courage, Caring and Community by Jack Canfield, Mark Victor Hansen, Arline McGraw Oberst, John T. Boal and Tom & Laura Lagana (Deerfield Beach, FL: Health Communications, Inc., 2002).

The Giving Box: Create a Tradition of Giving With Your Children by Fred Rogers (Philadephia: Running Press, 2000). For both adults and children over 7.

The Giving Family: Raising Our Children to Help Others by Susan Crites Price (Washington, DC: Council on Foundations, 2001).

Guerrilla Kindness: A Manual of Good Works, Kind Acts and Thoughtful Deeds by Gavin Whitsett (San Luis Obispo, CA: Impact Publishers, 1993).

Raising Kids Who Will Make a Difference: Helping Your Family Live With Integrity, Value Simplicity, and Care for Others by Susan V. Vogt (Chicago, IL: Loyola Press, 2002).

Teaching Your Kids to Care: How to Discover and Develop the Spirit of Charity in Your Children by Deborah Spaide (New York: Citadel Press, 1995).

Getting Started 2

Get the Family Involved

Finding a cause that appeals to every member of the family, locating an organization that welcomes kids, and preparing children for the challenges of volunteering takes thoughtful consideration and legwork. This chapter provides the practical tools your family will need to begin its quest.

First, you'll want to find an opportunity that suits all of your schedules, ages, skills, and personalities. Each family member will have his or her own ideas. Encourage all of your would-be volunteers to get involved in selecting the volunteer opportunity. The more each individual feels he or she has helped make the choice, the more committed everyone will be to making it work. The Family Volunteer Assessment Survey (Appendix page 176) can assist you in this process.

Consider these questions when beginning your search:

What skills, personality traits and talents does your family have to offer? Is your family active and physically fit? Maybe that could point to park service work or an outdoor environmental project. Is your teenage daughter skilled at working with children? This may suggest volunteering at a crisis nursery or mentoring a young boy or girl. Also consider your family's personalities. If your preschooler is outgoing and affectionate, she'd probably enjoy spending time at a nursing home. A shy child might be happier with a more behind-the-scenes job.

What do you want your family to learn from the experience? Most families volunteer because they want to teach the values of service and community involvement to their children. But what else would you like your children to gain? Do you want them to learn tolerance of those who come from different races or cultures? Then you might want to host a foreign student. Perhaps you'd like them to understand that not everyone has the material advantages you have. Then consider work in a homeless shelter. Think about the impact you'd like the volunteer work to have on your family members as you go about narrowing your search.

How much time are you able to commit? It's usually best to start small. A one-time commitment is a good way to begin; it allows your family to sample different types of volunteer activities without promising to be there for the long haul. Try a walk for charity, or cook a Thanksgiving dinner at a soup kitchen. Each chapter of this book includes a variety of simple and inexpensive volunteering options. Then take on something more regular if your family enjoyed the experience and has more time to give. But don't over commit. It's much easier and more comfortable to increase your volunteer time rather than having to cut back because you've taken on too much.

What causes or issues are important to your family? This means thinking about what matters to you. Are you focused on political issues or are you more social service-minded? Would you prefer to work with older adults or young children? Each chapter of this book focuses on a particular area of interest. Think about which topics your family feels most strongly about, and find a volunteer job that reflects those passions.

What are the ages of your children? Find a volunteer opportunity that's appropriate to your children's ages and maturity levels. Some activities might be too difficult for younger kids because they require a long attention span, higher-level skills, or emotional maturity. If you're uncertain about whether your child can handle a particular job, visit the agency and speak with the volunteer coordinator. But remember, families can design volunteer participation for any age child. Even babies and toddlers can take part in charity walks, meal deliveries, or visits to a nursing home. (See Appendix page 184 for volunteer projects appropriate for different ages.)

What times and locations are most convenient for your family? Are your children early risers or late sleepers? Does your daughter need an afternoon nap? Does your son count on going out with friends on Friday evenings? Are you too exhausted after a typical workday to tackle another commitment? Think about these patterns and preferences when choosing a volunteer activity. Also, pick a location that's convenient for you. You don't want the chore of getting there to interfere with your enthusiasm.

Do you want to volunteer with other families? One Sunday a month for many years, three families met at a local homeless shelter to cook and serve dinner. The children enjoyed spending time with one another, and volunteering provided the adults with a regular time each month to talk while they prepared the food. Some people feel that volunteering with other families enriches their experience. Others prefer to have the time alone with their immediate family. Discuss which option you prefer.

Kids, especially younger ones, may need your help articulating their ideas and opinions as you discuss family volunteering. Ask them questions and listen carefully to what they have to say. If your child seems overwhelmed by all the discussion, you may need to talk with your child alone to draw out more honest responses. Explain each of the issues in words your child can understand. Again, it's important to gather every family member's cooperation and enthusiasm as you begin to narrow down the possibilities.

A SUMMER TRANSFORMED

Zoey Albright, a Las Vegas mother, was determined that her boys, ages 7, 10, and 12, put aside their baseball mitts and Legos for part of the summer and get a taste of community service. She and her sons decided that because they missed spending time with their grandparents, who lived out of town, they wanted to try volunteering with seniors. The first nursing home Albright called wasn't interested in young volunteers. Then she found Vegas Valley, which welcomed her offer of some weekly company. On their first visit, says Albright, her kids were terrified. They had never spent time with people who were old or sick, and they reacted in horror when they saw a catheter bag strapped to a wheelchair. "Their initial reaction was to stick to me like glue," says Albright.

But she persevered, explaining to her sons the importance of respecting others despite their physical limitations. She also gave them practical suggestions for communicating with the residents. By the end of the summer, a transformation had occurred. The boys were off on their own, visiting room after room, reading to the residents, assisting in Bingo games, and pushing wheelchairs. Later, they announced that volunteering had been the summer's highlight.

Choose the Right Time Commitment

Often when we think of volunteering, we imagine assisting at an animal shelter once a month, sorting food at a food bank on certain evenings, or delivering meals to the homebound. This book is filled with examples of such opportunities. But there are also less structured ways for families to give their time, projects that enable families to volunteer whenever they choose. These informal ideas are ones your family initiates and pursues without an organization to sponsor your efforts. And you'll find dozens of examples of this type of volunteering in these pages. For example, you might clean up a local park or organize a fundraiser.

More structured volunteer efforts have the benefit of a standing commitment, which means volunteering is less likely to be pushed aside when the pressures of work, sports, or school intrude. Informal volunteering, on the other hand, enables families to volunteer at a time most convenient for their schedules, even if it changes often. Many families participate in both styles of volunteering. Your family can decide which type best fits your lifestyle and interests.

Finding the Right Opportunity

The quickest way to get started, of course, is to pick up the phone and call the organization that fits your volunteer criteria. For example, if your family has decided to spend time with animals, call animal shelters in your community to ask about volunteer positions. Other possibilities might include museums, historical societies, libraries, Meals on Wheels programs, schools, or local youth clubs. Check the Yellow Pages for a listing of such organizations near your home. In addition, the remaining chapters in this book provide ideas, contacts, organizations, and brainstorming tips to help you find the right volunteer opportunity.

If your family is still uncertain about where they'd like to volunteer, there are other resources to help you explore your options. Churches, temples, or synagogues often have service committees that offer volunteer opportunities. (In a 1999 survey by the Independent Sector, "Giving and Volunteering in America," one-third of family volunteers said they learned about their volunteer activity through a religious organization.)

In addition, almost every major city has a volunteer coordination office or volunteer clearinghouse or bureau that can provide leads for you. Check the phone book under "Volunteer Center," "Voluntary Action Center," or "Volunteer Bureau" or visit the Volunteer Center National Network at www.volunteerconnections.org. Provide your children's ages as well as your family's interests and availability. These organizations have large databases and can match you with specific volunteer opportunities. They'll supply you with the agencies and phone numbers and you can call any you want to pursue.

Ask your employer if it has a long-standing relationship with a charitable or community organization that could use your time and efforts. Or use your public library to find directories of nonprofit and social service organizations that may be a good fit for your family. Newspapers often have a weekly volunteer column, and your local parenting newspaper may be a good source of family volunteer opportunities.

Other Resources

Action Without Borders
www.contact.org

Check here for volunteer opportunities anywhere in the world, including overseas. The number of opportunities listed in each category is limited, however. Be certain to check out the section called "Kids & Teens."

City Cares
www.citycares.org
404-875-7334
1605 Peachtree Street, Suite 100, Atlanta, GA 30309

If your city is a member of this organization, you'll find an online calendar of volunteer opportunities specific to your area. These are often one-time opportunities that allow volunteers to get to know social service organizations and try out a variety of jobs, some specifically for families.

Give Spot
www.givespot.com

Find out more about volunteering, charities, donation sites, non-profits, and foundations at this all-inclusive website.

Hearts and Minds
www.heartsandminds.org

This site is rich in information, including descriptions of charitable organizations and inspirational quotes, but somewhat limited in terms of volunteer possibilities. It's interesting to peruse for ideas and inspiration.

Network for Good
www.networkforgood.org

Make a donation to charity, find out about volunteer opportunities, and learn to be an activist. Find resources and nonprofits in your family's area of interest.

Points of Light Foundation
Family Matters
www.pointsoflight.org
800-VOLUNTEER (800-865-8683)

Points of Light Foundation is a national non-profit dedicated to increasing volunteerism. Click on volunteer centers (or call the number above) to find the volunteer agency nearest you. Or go to "programs" and click on Family Matters to read about this organization's family volunteering initiative, especially National Family Volunteer Day. You can also click on FamilyCares (or visit www.familycares.org) to get ideas and inspiration for family volunteering. By clicking on Kids Care Clubs (www.kidscare.org), you'll get descriptions of volunteer projects specifically for children.

SERVEnet
www.servenet.org

This site lets you find opportunities by entering your zip code or you can create a "volunteer profile" to find volunteer projects that match your interests.

United Way
www.unitedway.org

Locate your local United Way website and click on "volunteer" to view the listings for your area.

Volunteer Match Online
www.volunteermatch.org

This website matches organizations looking for volunteers with people interested in making a volunteer commitment. It's not specifically for families, but there are hundreds of opportunities, some of which may work for you and your kids. Just enter your zip code.

Take Action

If you've decided on a one-time opportunity, it's usually a matter of either signing up (for example, to work at an arts and crafts fair) or simply doing the deed (bringing flowers to a neighbor). But if you're looking at a longer term commitment and have narrowed your search, it's important to get more detailed information from the agency or organization in question. (Use the "Family Volunteer Project Ideas" worksheet (Appendix page 177) to record what you learn.)

Here's how:
Call and ask for the volunteer coordinator or simply say, "My family is interested in volunteering. Whom should I speak with?" Explain your interest and ask lots of questions. Ask what services the organization provides, what volunteers do, and when they need workers. Let the coordinator know you want to volunteer as a family and give the ages of your children. Ask about training and orientation.

Many agencies have never used family volunteers, so they may be hesitant. But that doesn't mean it won't work for your family! If the agency expresses uncertainty, explain how your family would be a positive addition to its volunteer staff. Describe the advantages of youthful volunteers (for example, relating well to younger children or

NATIONAL FAMILY VOLUNTEER DAY

Each year since 1999, on the Saturday before Thanksgiving, the Points of Light Foundation has sponsored National Family Volunteer Day, a nationwide day of service for families who want to spend time in community service work together. A group of families in Green Bay, Wisconsin, spent the day assembling kits for the Einstein Project, which promotes science education. In Fort Lauderdale, Florida, families organized a neighborhood food drive. And volunteer families in Toledo, Ohio, cleaned and painted a family housing shelter and planted a rose garden. "We felt that family volunteering really needed a full day of impact to make the case that families are a valuable resource to nonprofits and community organizations in need of volunteers," says Diane Fabiyi-King, director of Family Matters, a program of the Points of Light Foundation dedicated to promoting family volunteering. The timing is ideal for families who are coming together for the holidays. The hope is that many of the participating families will make volunteering a year-round habit.

volunteering

delighting seniors). Also, organizations may be concerned about risk management, so emphasize that you'll be responsible for your children at all times.

Visit several places with your family to screen your options. Some may have orientation sessions, or you can make an appointment to speak with the volunteer coordinator and get a tour. Ask more questions to get a feel for the place. Trust your family's intuition about whether it's a comfortable working environment for all of you.

Make sure the agency really needs your help, that your volunteer job is making an important contribution, and that you'll be kept busy. When you meet with your supervisor or coordinator, did you feel as if you were treated as a valuable worker rather than as free help? Remember that you have the right to be treated with appreciation and respect.

If possible, ask a current or past volunteer about the pros and cons of his or her job. Be sure to ask about any problems as well as the advantages.

Research an organization before committing to it. Investigate the background and history of the agency. Read its newsletter. You might want to know the organization's goal or mission, how the group is funded, and how many volunteers are used.

Find out about the working conditions. (If you have small children, consider whether there is a bathroom and water supply readily available.) Ask if you would work with other volunteers. Also, be prepared for an interview or training time. You may be asked to fill out an application and describe your qualifications or background. A background check might also be required.

After doing your legwork, take some time to choose the opportunity that's right for your family. It's not necessary to go with the first place you see, but if you find a place that excites your family, go for it!

Prepare Your Kids

Once you've decided on a volunteer job, it's important to prepare your children for what to expect and how to behave. It is also important that everyone have a clear idea of why the family is spending its time volunteering. How you approach these issues can make a big difference in how excited your kids are about their new job. Here are some tips for getting all of you ready to begin your volunteering adventure.

Show enthusiasm. Tell your family how great it's going to be. Explain why you're looking forward to the experience. Enthusiasm is contagious and will help everyone approach the situation with a positive attitude.

Become educated. If appropriate, gather some background information before you begin the job. For example, if your family plans to spend time with foreign students, you might learn about their home country and get to know some words in their native language. The "Resources" sections of each chapter suggest books for parents and kids, and websites that will help introduce important concepts and spark conversation.

Determine whether taking part in the volunteer activity each time is required or optional. Some families make a commitment as a group to be available weekly or monthly for a volunteer project but decide that not every member needs to participate each time. So, for example, if you've decided to deliver meals, not all the children would need to accompany you on the route each week. Other families feel that all members should participate on every occasion. So you need to decide: What if your 13-year-old son wants to opt out of working at the children's museum one month? What if your daughter has a soccer game or your preschooler is invited to a birthday party? It's best to discuss how you'll handle possible conflicts before they arise.

Describe what will happen. Explain as closely as you can exactly how things will go when you arrive or begin your volunteer job. "When we get there, we'll unload our groceries. Dad will start chopping vegetables, and you and I will set the table."

Let them know how they're expected to behave. Spend some time discussing appropriate rules of conduct and any special safety considerations. If the agency has provided any rules or guidelines, review these with your children.

Explain why this job is important. Everyone likes to know that they're making a difference, children included. Explain that collecting and donating books means that children who might never own a book may now be inspired to read.

Understand the Commitment

Finding a volunteer job is only the beginning. If you've chosen to undertake an ongoing commitment, it's important that your family volunteering experience continue to be fun and meaningful. To make it work for the long haul, here are some things you can do:

Learn more about your position. Talk to your supervisor about what to do in difficult circumstances. Ask what to do if you can't make it.

Take the volunteer position seriously. Follow the rules and do your best. Be there even when life gets hectic. And be on time. It's important to be reliable even if it's a volunteer position. This sends an important message to your children about responsibility. But also expect respect in return. If staff people are rude or don't say thank you, let someone know.

Talk about the volunteer experience with your family. Share the disappointments and challenges of the work with your children and educate them about the issues at hand. Why are there homeless people? Why is it important to recycle? Why do we need a neighborhood watch group?

Continue to explain the benefits to the people you serve. It's important for children (and the rest of us) that we understand why our work is making a difference. "Maintaining this trail means that hundreds of visitors will be able to continue to enjoy this park."

Be patient with your children's efforts. Praise your child for her efforts rather than being critical of less-than-perfect results. Keep in mind that although your children may seem a little unproductive at first—and even in the way sometimes—if they remain enthusiastic about what they're doing, it could mean years of helpful community service in the future.

Show your children what they're learning by volunteering. Discuss what skills all of you have gained from volunteering and how each of you has benefited from the experience. This is an important way to keep your kids excited about what they're doing. Share compliments you receive from other workers or people you serve. Tell your child that you see him exhibiting a growing sense of responsibility.

Have a good time. Your family will do a better job and stick with it longer if you're enjoying your time together. So do what you can to make that happen. Maybe you could invite your child's friend to help out, or stop for ice cream on the way home.

Take time to reflect. This can occur while you're in the midst of the volunteer experience and after the project ends. Pose provocative questions to your family. How would you describe the people you met? What was the best/worst/most memorable thing that happened? How did this project affect you? What did you learn from it? What would you do differently next time? Encourage all family members to participate, and acknowledge each person's contribution to the discussion. Use the "Reflections" worksheet (Appendix page 178) to record your family's thoughts. Parents might invite younger children to draw pictures relating to their experience or create a photo album or scrapbook.

People-to-People Ties 3

One volunteer idea that requires absolutely no skill or experience is, quite simply, your friendship. You can visit an isolated senior eager for conversation and companionship, mentor a child, or provide transportation and child care to a family newly arrived from another country. Build a relationship with a family in poverty or become an e-mail correspondent with a nursing home resident. Your family will learn that people's differences—in culture and language, age, income level, or way of life—don't really make much difference at all. And remember, even the smallest contribution can mean a new friend for you and your family and a sense of hope and possibility for someone who's struggling. Here are some ways your family can reach out to others.

Work With Senior Citizens

My husband's grandmother, 96, tells the story of how her mother and uncle got lost on the prairie for three days and nights when they were just four and six years old, respectively. She describes how they survived by sleeping in abandoned barns and drinking from puddles, and how they were rescued by their father as they lay near death. She also tells about life on their farm, the Czech pastries her grandmother baked, and why her two marriages failed. These stories are one of the reasons our family loves to visit Grandma. Another is that she is so appreciative of our company.

When families spend time with seniors, everyone benefits. Older people get a chance to share their life adventures and enjoy the exuberance of youth, while younger generations profit from the wisdom and experience of age. You'll also be doing your part to help the different generations understand one another better.

There are many ways your family can volunteer with the elderly. You can volunteer for a one-time event, or forge an ongoing relationship with a nursing home resident

(According to The Senior Source, a nonprofit in Dallas, Texas, 60% of residents never have a visitor [www.theseniorsource.org/ pages/Statinfo_Nursing.html]). Or create your own job, such as teaching nursing home residents computer skills. And don't forget elderly people who live at home. They need companionship as well as practical help to maintain their house or apartment.

To get started, look in the Yellow Pages under Senior Citizens' Services or Nursing Homes.

Ideas for Working With Seniors

- ☼ Assist an elderly person living at home with laundry, yard work, and house cleaning. If you don't know of a senior who needs help, contact an organization in your area that serves the elderly. This can be a one-time commitment or a weekly or monthly affair.

- ☼ Adopt-a-Grandparent. Ask the volunteer coordinator at a local nursing home about the process for matching families and residents, and then choose an elderly person to visit regularly. Ideally, you'll be paired with someone who has similar interests. Spend time talking, reading, writing letters, playing games, and simply strolling. This is a volunteer opportunity that families with children of any age can enjoy.

- ☼ Initiate or help with activities at a nursing home or senior center.

  - Give a party. Who doesn't love a celebration? Work with the staff to arrange a date and time. Plan the menu, music, games, entertainment, or activities. Make decorations.

  - Assist with celebrations, games, and outings. There is always a need for extra hands at special events.

  - Plan and carry out a craft night. Find out what day and time would be most convenient. Then think of an idea for a craft, work out the steps for completing the project, buy the materials, and clean up.

  - Share a hobby. Maybe your family would enjoy doing crossword puzzles with residents, gardening, or listening to jazz. Ask the staff which seniors might enjoy the hobby your family would like to share.

  - Help with Bingo. Your family can pass out prizes, call numbers, assist residents, and transport them to and from their rooms.

  - Perform a family talent show. Can anyone in your family sing, dance, play a musical instrument or juggle? If so, you can entertain elderly residents and provide a pleasant distraction. Arrange a date and time with the staff. Invite your children's friends or another family to join the show.

- Escort residents of a nursing home on walks. Push a wheelchair or provide an arm for support so that residents can enjoy being outdoors or in the halls.

- Be a lunch buddy. Once each month, take your family to a local nursing home to have lunch with a resident.

☼ Become an e-mail pen pal with a resident of a nursing home. Call a nursing home for the name of an individual who would like to correspond with your family. Or check out Elders Without Walls, an organization that facilitates e-mail correspondence between residents of assisted living facilities and the general public.

Elders Without Walls
www.elderswithoutwalls.com

☼ Make deliveries to nursing home residents or elderly neighbors. Here are some deliveries that are sure to brighten someone's day.

- Make gifts to give, such as a calendar, sun-catcher, table centerpiece, bird feeder, bookmark, or decorative pot for a plant. For more ideas, check out craft books from the library.

- Make brownies, soup, or a loaf of bread to share. There's nothing like a gift of food to bring people together.

- Bring fresh flowers from your garden. Help beautify someone's home or room with a bouquet.

- Bring books or tapes from the library. Does your family love books? Then you probably make frequent trips to the library. Ferret out the book lovers at your local nursing home, and offer to pick up and return tapes and books for them. Family members can read some of the same books and take time to discuss them when making pick-ups and drop-offs.

☼ Bring your family pet for a visit with nursing home residents. A visit with a pet offers people companionship and love. It gives them something to look forward to and relieves loneliness. In addition, it can be a conversation starter. Check with the facility before bringing a pet, and approach each resident first to be certain he or she wants to interact with your pet. The organizations listed below will provide information on evaluating and certifying your pet for visits.

Delta Society
www.deltasociety.org
425-226-7357

Therapy Dogs
www.therapydogs.com
877-843-7364

Dog Play
www.dog-play.com/therapy.html

☀ Be a calling buddy to an elderly person. Call periodically and be available if your elderly friend needs to talk. Regular contact can ease loneliness and depression. Members of the family can take turns making the calls.

☀ Invite an elderly person to your home for a meal. This is a simple gesture that can bring an evening of pleasure to an isolated senior and add some new conversation to your family dinner. It can be a one-time event or a once-a-month ritual.

☀ Take nursing home residents or homebound seniors to visit their friends or drive friends to visit them. Or offer to drive them to medical appointments or the grocery store. Many seniors have difficulty with transportation for errands or appointments. Your kids can come along for the ride, and the driving time can be an opportunity to visit and enjoy one another's company.

☀ Help elderly people write their life stories to pass down to their grandchildren and great grandchildren. Here are some suggestions for getting started.

● Listen to and record stories each time you visit. When you have a dozen or so, type them and take them to a copy center to have them bound. Add pictures if you have any. Then give the "book" as a gift.

● Buy a blank book and write a question on each page for the person to answer. ("When was the first time you met your spouse?") Record the response. Continue to add questions as you hear the details of the person's life.

DOG DAYS

Greyhounds, which are large, gentle dogs, are the perfect height for wheelchairs. The Wilkins-Reed family knows this fact because once a month, Margo Wilkins and her four daughters, ages 5 to 13, take their pet greyhound into a local Memphis nursing home to visit with residents. It's a four-story building, and when the kids have the energy, the family goes to every room on each floor, asking from the doorway, "Do you like dogs?" before stepping in for a visit. Many of the elderly people use the visit as an opportunity to tell stories about their own pets, talk about visits to the racetrack, or simply have a conversation. Even 5-year-old Thea happily interacts with the residents. "She feels really comfortable saying, 'Do you want to pet the dog?' and gently taking their hand off their laps and putting it on the head of the dog," says Wilkins. "All of the kids have become accepting of people's differences."

Volunteering

("What did you do when you returned from military service?") You can decorate the cover with old photographs.

- Make a timeline that records the major events of the person's life. This project often sparks memories and stories.

- Write captions for the person's photos. Simply write down his or her description of the image and paste it on the back of the photo.

Capturing Memories
www.capturingmemories.com
866-595-9662
9228 209th Street, Vashon, WA 98070
This website offers a more detailed look at these ideas and more.

Resources for Volunteering With Senior Citizens

Books for Kids

Let's Talk About When Someone You Love Is in a Nursing Home by Diana Star Helmer (New York: Rosen Publishing Group, 2003). Ages 3-8. This book provides a simple understanding of what nursing homes are like and why people need to go to them. It also describes what children can do when they visit, such as give hugs and play games.

Miss Tizzy by Libba Moore Gray, illustrated by Jada Rowland (New York: Simon and Schuster, 1998). Ages 4-8. The eccentric Miss Tizzy loves the neighborhood children, and they return her devotion when she becomes ill.

The Old Woman Who Loved to Read by John Winch (New York: Holiday House, 1998). Ages 4-7. A simple narrative about an older woman who escapes to the country to find some quiet for reading, but winds up plowing the fields, tending a lamb, and repairing her barn. A light and amusing, non-stereotypical view of an older woman.

Sitti's Secrets by Naomi Shihab Nye, illustrated by Nancy Carpenter (New York: Simon and Schuster, 1997). Ages 5-8. A young girl visits her grandmother in a Palestinian village. Their love transcends differences in language and culture.

Wilfrid Gordon McDonald Partridge by Mem Fox, illustrated by Julie Vivas (La Jolla, CA: Kane/Miller Book Publishers, 1995). Ages 5-8. This boy with four names lives next door to a nursing home and has made friends with the residents. Heartwarming.

Kids and Grandparents: An Activity Book by Ann Love and Jane Drake, illustrated by Heather Collins (New York: Kids Can Press, 2000). Ages 5 and up. Some of these activities are for children and elderly people who share the same family, but most can be modified. The projects include recipes, memory activities, crafts, and games.

Old People, Frogs, and Albert by Nancy Hope Wilson, illustrated by Marcy D. Ramsey (New York: Farrar, Straus and Giroux, 1999). Ages 7-9. Albert, a fourth-grader who struggles with reading, learns to overcome his fear of the Pine Manor Nursing Home when his reading tutor, Mr. Spear, takes up residence there following a stroke.

Linnea in Monet's Garden by Christina Bjork, illustrated by Lena Anderson (New York: Farrar, Straus, and Giroux, 1987). Ages 9-12. Linnea and her elderly neighbor, Mr. Bloom, visit Paris and Monet's garden in Giverny. A delightful story of the relationship of a child and her older friend.

The Cay by Theodore Taylor (New York: Random House, 2002). Young adult. Phillip is stranded on a Caribbean Island with an older West Indian man named Timothy, on whom he must depend to survive.

The Friends by Kazumi Yumoto, translated by Cathy Hirano (New York: Random House, 1998). Young adult. The story of a friendship between three Japanese boys and a wise older man.

Tiger, Tiger, Burning Bright by Ronald Koertge (New York: Orchard Books, 1994). Young adult. Thirteen-year-old Jesse tries to keep his mother from realizing that his beloved grandfather, Pappy, is losing his memory.

Organizations and Websites

The Eldercare Locator
www.eldercare.gov
800-677-1116
The U.S. Department of Health and Human Services Administration on Aging provides this nationwide directory assistance to help locate local support resources for the elderly. This is a good way to locate your nearest nursing home or senior center.

Faith in Action
www.fiavolunteers.org
877-324-8411
This is a volunteer movement that unites religious groups and community organizations to help the elderly and chronically ill. The website lists organizations around the country that serve these populations.

Help the Aged Schools Programme
www.helptheaged.org.uk/schools
The cartoon characters will get children thinking about important issues relating to the elderly. Some of the terms used on this British-based site may confuse American children.

Little Brothers, Friends of the Elderly
www.littlebrothers.org
312-829-3055
954 W. Washington Blvd., 5th Floor, Chicago, IL 60607

Volunteers work with the elderly in nine cities across the country, including Boston, Minneapolis, Omaha, Chicago, Philadelphia, and San Francisco.

10 TIPS FOR SUCCESSFUL NURSING HOME VISITS

1. Prepare your children for what they might see, including wheelchairs, catheters, and some elderly people who are loud, confused, or nonresponsive.
2. Read some books about older people before you go. Discuss stereotypes and the importance of respect.
3. Assure your children that it's fine to ask questions, but to respect the feelings and privacy of the residents.
4. Don't visit if your children are ill.
5. Make arrangements to visit ahead of time and always come when you say you will.
6. Plan ahead what you're going to do when you visit.
7. Knock first and ask permission before entering a resident's room.
8. If you bring a food to share, be sure it is something the person can eat. Some people have dietary restrictions.
9. If you start a project with a resident, bring all necessary supplies. If the project isn't completed when it's time for your family to leave, clean up thoroughly and bring it back next time.
10. Don't be in a hurry. Take time with each person your family interacts with.

volunteering

Aid the Sick

The 1998 film *Patch Adams* told the true story of an unconventional doctor who believed that pleasure, humor, and friendship were essential components of healing. "What so many sick people in this world suffer from—loneliness, boredom and fear—can't be cured with a pill," the real-life Adams says in Patch Adams' Story (www.patchadams.com/story3.html). The answer, he maintains, is conversation and laughter, and that's just the kind of medicine volunteers can provide. Your family can entertain hospital patients, offer support to their families, or hand out coffee at a blood drive. (Interestingly, Adams also maintains that service to others is the most effective way to combat one's own problems.)

If you have budding doctors in your midst, volunteering can also be an ideal way to explore career options in health care. This type of volunteer work can be intensely rewarding, but some family members may find it difficult to be around adults and children who are ill. Discuss this with your family, and be certain to visit the hospital or clinic before you commit to volunteer there. Also, keep in mind that hospitals usually require screening and sometimes training before you can begin volunteering. Check the Yellow Pages for medical facilities near you, or ask your family doctor for suggestions.

Ideas for Helping Sick Children and Their Families

☼ Help out in the pediatric ward of a local hospital or in a nearby children's hospital. The time you spend playing with a child can give his or her parents a much-needed break and give the child some distraction from boredom and discomfort. Here are some things you can do together:

- Bring a Polaroid camera and take some silly pictures.

- Make a book together. The child can tell a story that you write down, and then illustrate it.

- Play cards or board games.

- Give a juggling or Yo-Yo demonstration.

- Bring a tape recorder and record the child singing or answering interview questions.

- Work on puzzles or bring a construction toy to build together.

- Have a sing-a-long.

- Dress up as clowns. Your whole family can "clown around" for sick kids.

- Take around a cart with books or toys to bedridden children. Although most pediatric wards have libraries and play rooms, some children aren't able to access them. Ask if your family can bring toys and books to these kids. Then spend time with the kids playing games, reading, or doing puzzles.

- Read your family's favorite books. Ask your children to choose their best-loved books, and take them to a hospital and read to the sick kids. Your younger children can listen to the stories; the older ones can help read.

- Put on a puppet show. Your family will have fun and you'll brighten the day of a lot of sick kids.

- Conduct a craft activity. Plan an activity that can be enjoyed by children of a wide range of ages. Check with the hospital's volunteer coordinator to arrange a place and time. Bring along the necessary materials. For craft ideas, check your local library or visit http://home.att.net/~DLeddy/kids.html or www.makingfriends.com.

- Hold and rock babies. Babies who are premature or hospitalized for other reasons need touch and comfort. And hospitals don't always have enough staff to go around. However, be aware that hospitals may require a minimum age of 16 (or even older) for this job. Check with your local medical facility to see if your family can help.

☼ Read to children in the waiting room of a hospital or medical clinic. Choose a "story corner" and read books to young children while they are waiting to see the doctor or waiting to spend time with a sick brother, sister, or parent.

☼ Tape children's books and take them to kids in the hospital. Read your favorite stories into a tape recorder. Make sound effects, change voices for each character, and add life to the story! Then donate the tapes to a children's hospital or deliver them in person to kids in the pediatric ward.

☼ Collect and donate children's books to a hospital's pediatric ward. Everybody has children's books around the house that the kids have outgrown. Find ones in good condition and donate them to the nearest hospital.

☼ Help at a Ronald McDonald House. These "houses that

HOUSE WORK

Maureen Koteles, who lives in Rockford, Illinois, is a board member for Ronald McDonald House Charities. Several times each year she makes the hour and a half drive to the Ronald McDonald House in Madison, Wisconsin, for meetings. And whenever school is not in session, her daughters, Lauren, 17, and Brittany, 13, accompany her. While their mother is involved with the board, the girls take on a variety of tasks at the house, including making cookies, stuffing envelopes, preparing packets for the guests—whatever needs to be done. According to Coleen Flad, the volunteer director at the 18-bedroom house, family volunteers with children over 12 are enthusiastically welcomed. Chores might include checking in families, helping with meal preparation, providing tours, answering phones, or cleaning and preparing rooms. "Just picture what needs to be done in your own house before company comes. Except in this case there are 18 families to get ready for," says Flad.

volunteering

love built" are havens for families whose children are in area hospitals. They provide lodging, meals and support. You can help with donations, fundraising, event planning, meal preparation, and house maintenance.

Ronald McDonald House Charities
www.rmhc.com
630-623-7048
One Kroc Drive, Oak Brook, IL 60523

☼ Befriend a family whose child is in the hospital. You can provide invaluable support, companionship, and practical assistance. If the family is in town temporarily to be near their child, your family can provide transportation for grocery shopping and recreational activities. You might also transport patients and their family members and friends to and from the airport and provide information about the city or town where you live.

☼ Befriend a chronically ill child in his or her home. Play and interact with the child and provide support to the parents. Contact Easter Seals or your local hospital to be matched with a child in need.

☼ Send mail to sick children. Visit www.hugsandhope.com for the names and stories of hospitalized children who could use your message of support and encouragement.

☼ Your children can join the Peter Pan Birthday Club and raise money for a local children's hospital.

Peter Pan Children's Fund
www.peterpanchildrensfund.org
914-764-9585
P.O. Box 388, Pound Ridge, NY 10576

Ideas for Helping Sick Adults and Their Families

☼ Volunteer at a hospital.

- Provide music at bedside or in groups. Does your family have some musical talent to share? Entertain sick children or adults with a mini-concert.

- Visit with patients. Many people don't have visitors and become isolated and lonely. Your family can sit and talk, play cards or games, or help them write letters.

- Deliver flowers and mail. Call the volunteer coordinator at a local hospital and ask if your family can make deliveries together. Spend time talking to patients if they're well enough.

- Help out at hospital-sponsored community functions.

- Lend a hand at a flower or gift shop, patient library, or the information desk.

☼ Walk (or run) to fight disease. Many organizations use walks or runs to increase awareness of a certain disease—and raise badly needed funds. This can be a simple one-time event that any member of the family can enjoy, or you can make it an annual family tradition. Put your little ones in a stroller, get some exercise, and contribute to a worthy cause. Contact the following organizations for more information.

		Contacts
Breast cancer	www.raceforthecure.com 800-462-9273	
Juvenile diabetes	www.jdf.org 800-533-CURE (2873)	
Leukemia and lymphoma	www.lightthenight.org 800-955-4572	
Parkinson's disease	www.unitywalk.org 866-789-9255	
AIDS	www.aidswalk.org	
Asthma and lung disease	www.lungusa.org 212-315-8700	
Multiple sclerosis	www.nmss.org 800-Fight MS (800-344-4867)	
Alzheimer's disease	www.alz.org 800-272-3900	

☼ Form a special relationship with a person with AIDS. Provide practical help, such as helping the person get to medical appointments or support groups, or running errands. Offer emotional support. Spend time together reading, talking, walking, and enjoying each other's company.

☼ Make a meal for a family whose loved one is sick or in the hospital. When families are facing a medical problem or even in the midst of a positive life event, such as having a baby, it's hard to find time to grocery shop or cook. A home-cooked meal can be a comfort. Pack the meal in disposable dishes so no returns are necessary.

☼ Help cancer patients. You can collect hats and donate them for adults and children who have lost their hair from chemotherapy. Or drive cancer patients to their treatments. Call the American Cancer Society for more information.

American Cancer Society
www.cancer.org
800-ACS-2345

☼ Become a blood donor or help with a blood drive. Blood donations help sustain life, and the only source is volunteer blood donors. Although you must be 17 years old to donate blood, younger children can help out in other ways. Your family can work as greeters or "hosts" at a blood bank, help ensure that the donors are comfortable, and bring them fluids and snacks. Your care will encourage donors to return. You can also make phone calls to recruit blood donors. Training and calling lists can be provided by the blood bank. Contact your local Red Cross or call a local blood bank for information.

American Red Cross
www.redcross.org
800-448-3543

☼ Organize first-aid training for a school or community group. Contact your local chapter of the Red Cross or the American Heart Association for more information.

American Red Cross
www.redcross.org
866-GET-INFO; 202-303-4498

American Heart Asssociation
www.americanheart.org
800-242-8721

Resources for Aiding the Sick

Books for Kids

Franklin Goes to the Hospital by Paulette Bourgeois, illustrated by Brenda Clark (New York: Scholastic Inc., 2000). Ages 4-8. Franklin's visit to the hospital to repair a cracked shell can introduce young children to all aspects of a hospital stay.

Going to the Hospital by Fred Rogers, photographs by Jim Judkis (New York: G.P. Putnam's Sons, 1997). Ages 4-8. A comforting look at hospitals and hospital procedures through the experiences of two young children.

Magic School Bus: Inside the Human Body by Joanna Cole, illustrated by Bruce Degen (New York: Scholastic, Inc., 1990). Ages 6-9. For kids interested in medicine, a fun and informative journey through the human body.

Sadako and the Thousand Paper Cranes by Eleanor Coerr, paintings by Ronald Himmler (New York: Puffin, 1999). Ages 8-12. A young Hiroshima girl in the 1940s is sick with leukemia from atom bomb radiation. Legend says that if she folds a thousand paper cranes she'll get healthy; she decides to try. A true story of courage.

Deenie by Judy Blume (New York: Simon and Schuster, 1991). Young adult. A young girl copes with scoliosis.

Just What the Doctor Ordered: The History of American Medicine by Brandon Marie Miller (Minneapolis: Lerner Publications Company, 1997). Young adult. Interesting and informative look back at American medicine.

Teens Face to Face With Chronic Illness by Suzanne LeVert (New York: Simon and Schuster, 1993). Young adult. The medical information may be somewhat dated, but it's a helpful overview of several chronic illnesses from a teen perspective, including asthma, arthritis, and hemophilia.

Young People and Chronic Illness: True Stories, Help, and Hope by Kelly Huegel (Minneapolis: Free Spirit Publishing, 1998). Young adult. Teens can learn about others their age who are struggling with diabetes, epilepsy, and other chronic illnesses.

Organizations and Websites

CDC National AIDS Hotline
800-342-AIDS (2437)
Call for information on volunteer opportunities with AIDS patients in your area.

Pediatric AIDS Foundation
www.pedaids.org
888-499-HOPE (4673)
1140 Connecticut Avenue, NW, Suite 200, Washington, DC 20036
Facts on pediatric AIDs and links to sites that provide information on HIV/AIDS.

Reach Out and Read
Reach Out and Read National Center
www.reachoutandread.org
617-629-8042
29 Mystic Avenue, Somerville, MA 02145
This national program encourages pediatricians to make literacy a significant part of their patient care. One component has volunteers reading to children in waiting rooms of clinics and hospitals. Contact this group for good information on child literacy, to see if there's a chapter near you, or to get information on starting a program in your community.

Reach Out to People With Disabilities

Nineteen-year-old Joanna Dee is an accomplished dancer who has performed for dozens of audiences. But nowhere is she more applauded and appreciated than when she's volunteered to waltz and whirl with a group of people with developmental disabilities at a dance sponsored by the St. Louis Association for Retarded Citizens (SLARC). From the time she was in seventh grade until she graduated from high school, Joanna and about 20 other students, as well as Joanna's mother, Susan, a teacher at her school, looked forward once each year to dancing, socializing, and enjoying the company of adults with mental retardation. "It's phenomenal," says Susan. "Kids who would never dance at a school dance lose all their inhibitions. The students are just beaming the whole time."

Your family can help either adults or children with disabilities become less isolated and more engaged in everyday activities, such as answering mail, going shopping, or participating in sports. In return, you and your children will gain a renewed understanding of your own challenges and strengths.

Talk to your kids before pursuing this kind of volunteering. Explain that there are some things that people with disabilities can't do, or do differently. For example, some people can't move their arms or legs. Others have trouble hearing or seeing. Some have difficulty learning. You might also talk about the kinds of equipment those with disabilities use and how they are able to compensate to complete everyday tasks. Discussing these issues ahead of time can help ensure a comfortable experience for everyone.

Ideas for Reaching Out to People With Disabilities

- ☼ Form a friendship with someone with intellectual disabilities. Call a residential treatment center for the developmentally disabled in your area or see if Best Buddies, an organization dedicated to forming relationships between individuals with intellectual disabilities and students, individuals, or families, has an office near you.

  Best Buddies International, Inc.
  www.bestbuddies.org
  305-374-2233, 800-89-BUDDY
  100 SE Second Street, #1900, Miami, FL 33131

- ☼ Form an e-mail relationship with an individual with intellectual disabilities.

  e-Buddies Headquarters
  www.ebuddies.org
  202-266-2295
  401 Ninth Street, NW, Suite 750, Washington, DC 20004

- ☼ Include a person with a disability on family outings. Contact a residential facility for people with disabilities and ask about residents who might enjoy an outing. Take simple trips to the market, a movie, or the park.

☼ Assist in a group home for the disabled. Help out with activities, everyday tasks, or special events.

☼ Volunteer to help with Special Olympics. Volunteers can provide transportation, assist food service workers, take part in telephone campaigns, distribute materials for Special Olympics events, or serve as greeters, escorts, or cheerleaders.

Special Olympics
www.specialolympics.org
202-628-3630

☼ Provide respite care for children or adults with disabilities. Any caregiver who provides constant care to a family member would appreciate a break. You can help by providing temporary care (for example, one night or a weekend) for the child or adult. It relieves a family's stress and fatigue and prevents burnout.

ARCH National Respite Network and Resource Center
Chapel Hill Training-Outreach Project
www.chtop.com/archbroc.htm
800-473-1727 ext.222
800 Eastowne Drive, Suite 105, Chapel Hill, NC 27514
The website contains excellent information on respite care and crisis nursery care. ARCH also operates the National Respite Locator Service to help people locate respite care services in their area.

☼ Help someone who is visually impaired. Volunteers are often needed to help do chores, read mail, or provide transportation. Look under "Blind Services" in the Yellow Pages for organizations that may be looking for help.

☼ Help produce "talking books" for the blind, dyslexic, and physically disabled. Volunteers may also be needed to record the weekly newspaper, record materials requested by patrons, and help shelve tapes and materials at "talking book centers." Contact your local library for information.

☼ Help out at a camp for children with disabilities. You may lead craft projects, teach swimming, or help with entertainment. To find a camp in your area, visit www.kidscamps.com or call your local Easter Seals.

Resources for Reaching Out to People With Disabilities

Books for Kids

Let's Talk About It: Extraordinary Friends by Fred Rogers, photographs by Jim Judkis (New York: Puffin Books, 2000). Ages 4-8. Children meet children and adults with disabilities and get suggestions on how to make friends with them.

Someone Special, Just Like You by Tricia Brown, photographs by Fran Ortiz (New York: Henry Holt and Company, 1995). Ages 4-8. Photographs and simple text that give the message that children with disabilities are just like other kids.

Susan Laughs by Jeanne Willis, illustrated by Tony Ross (New York: Henry Holt and Company, 2000). Ages 4-8. Rhyming couplets help readers understand that kids with disabilities are kids first. Children will identify with this young girl in a wheelchair.

Be Good to Eddie Lee by Virginia Fleming, illustrated by Floyd Cooper (New York: Putnam Publishing Group, 1997). Ages 5-9. The story of a friendship between a young girl and a boy with Downs Syndrome.

Just Kids: Visiting a Class for Children With Special Needs by Ellen Senisi (New York: Dutton Children's Books, 1998). Ages 6-12. Children learn about a variety of disabilities through the experiences of Cindy, a second-grader who is placed in a class of kids with epilepsy, autism, and other special needs.

Deaf Child Crossing by Marlee Matlin (New York: Simon and Schuster, 2002). Ages 9-12. The story of the friendship between a deaf child and a hearing child.

The Disability Rights Movement by Deborah Kent (New York: Grolier Publishing, 1997). Ages 9-12. A narrative history of the struggle for people with disabilities to be heard.

Mirror, Mirror on the Wall: The Diary of Bess Brennan by Barry Denenberg (New York: Scholastic, Inc., 2002). Ages 9-12. Set in the 1930s, the 12-year-old heroine is blinded in a sledding accident and must learn how to adjust.

Extraordinary People With Disabilities by Deborah Kent and Kathryn A. Quinlan (New York: Grolier Publishing, 1997). Young adult. Brief stories of 48 famous people who dealt with disabilities, including Thomas Edison, Theodore Roosevelt, and Tom Cruise.

Izzy, Willy-Nilly by Cynthia Voigt (New York: Simon and Schuster, 1995). Young adult. Fifteen-year-old Isobel loses her leg in a car accident and learns to cope with her disability.

Petey by Ben Mikaelson (New York: Hyperion Press, 2000). Young adult. Petey, who has cerebral palsy, is misdiagnosed as an infant and raised in a mental institution. This is the story of his struggles and friendships, especially with a lonely boy named Trevor.

Organizations and Websites

The Arc of the United States
www.thearc.org
301-565-3842
1010 Wayne Avenue, Suite 650, Silver Spring, MD 20910
An organization supporting people with mental retardation and related developmental disabilities and their families.

Easter Seals
www.easter-seals.org.
800-221-6827
230 West Monroe Street, Suite 1800, Chicago, IL 60606
Provides help for people with disabilities, including child care, camping and recreation, adult care, and job training and employment. You can write, call, or visit the website to get volunteer information in your area.

National Federation for the Blind
www.nfb.org
Be sure to visit the section of the website called "Questions Kids Ask about Blindness," which contains fascinating information about living with blindness.

Parent Advocacy Coalition for Education Rights (PACER)
www.pacer.org
800-537-2237
Helps children and young adults with disabilities and their families. Ask them about what services and resources are available in your area.

Recording for the Blind and Dyslexic
www.rfbd.org.
800-803-7201 (volunteer information)
20 Roszel Road, Princeton, NJ 08540
This organization uses readers and a variety of other volunteers. Contact it to find the office nearest you.

United Cerebral Palsy
www.ucpa.org
800-872-5827
1660 L Street, NW, Suite 700, Washington, DC 20036
Visit this website to find the cerebral palsy support organization in your area.

Lend Support to Children and Families

Kids like spending time with other kids, so volunteer opportunities that involve youngsters are almost certain to delight your own children. Some of the projects listed below (for instance, becoming a foster family) require a large commitment of time and energy. But others are simple gestures that can be equally rewarding. And when children who are volunteering find out that other kids—even if they live in a shelter, with a foster family, or in a different part of the country—also like to play basketball and ride bikes, they begin to think of all kids as being pretty much the same.

Strong families mean healthy children and healthy communities. You can help kids by supporting their families in different ways. Many parents are lonely and are seeking contact with other parents. Others may be looking for a healthy family model for their children. Volunteer families not only provide emotional support, but also help problem solve, provide transportation, and offer child care or other practical assistance. Best of all, by helping other families, you'll be strengthening your own, as well.

Ideas for Supporting Children and Families

☼ Mentor a child. Include a disadvantaged child in your family's activities several times a month. The organizations that match families and kids emphasize that the activities don't need to cost money. Bake cookies together, go fishing, or play board games. These mentorships can make a big difference in the life of a child. Contact the organizations listed below or your local YMCA for more information.

Big Brothers Big Sisters of America National Office
www.bbbsa.org
215-567-7000
230 N. 13th Street, Philadelphia, PA 19107
This is the oldest and largest mentoring organization in the United States.

MENTOR/The National Mentoring Partnership
www.mentoring.org
703-224-2200
1600 Duke Street, Suite 300, Alexandria, VA 22314
Find dozens of mentoring organizations in your area that you can contact to volunteer.

☼ Play with kids after school. Many communities with after-school programs for children are eager for some help. Your family might plan craft projects, share a talent, go on field trips, or help with homework. If there is no program in your area, organize one at a local park or school. Or get involved with Boys & Girls Clubs of America, which has chapters in all 50 states.

Boys & Girls Clubs of America
www.bgca.org
800-854-CLUB

☼ For each family member's birthday, pick out a gift for a child in need. Make each birthday in your family an occasion to help others by giving as well as receiving gifts.

☼ Repair old bikes. Are members of your family mechanically inclined? Have friends and neighbors donate used bikes. Make the necessary repairs before donating them to children who can't afford their own bicycles.

☼ Make a life book for a child in foster care. Collect pictures of a foster child's friends, relatives, and teachers. Have them each write something to the child and compile it in a book. This can be comforting to a child who's in transition and needs a sense of connectedness. Contact your county's social services department for guidance.

☼ Host a foreign student. Providing a home for a student from another culture for 5-10 months is a fun way to offer your children some cross-cultural awareness. Host families can live anywhere—big city or small town—and have children of any age. Most students have some knowledge of English. Some families form life-long relationships with their students. The students generally have their own spending money and health insurance. They need their own bed, two meals each day, and your family's kindness and support. Here are some organizations that match foreign students and host families.

American Field Service (AFS)
http://usa.afs.org
800-AFS-INFO

American Intercultural Student Exchange
www.aise.com
800-SIBLING
7720 Herschel Avenue, La Jolla, California 92037

EF Foundation for Foreign Study
www.effoundation.org
800-44-SHARE
EF Center Boston, One Education Street, Cambridge, MA 02141

ASA International
www.asainternational.com
800-303-4100
7119 Church Avenue, Ben Avon, PA 15202

☼ Plan an event for National Family Week. For the last 30 years, the Alliance for Families and Children has set aside the week of Thanksgiving to celebrate, honor, and strengthen families. You can involve your community by organizing a family-related activity.

Alliance for Children and Families
www.nationalfamilyweek.org
800-221-2681

☼ Care for a foster child. Foster families are always needed to provide temporary homes for children waiting to be returned to their parents or placed for adoption.

This is a huge commitment, of course, but even if you can't take in a foster child, there are other ways you can help. Your family can volunteer to assist with parties for foster children or provide birthday or holiday gifts. Volunteer drivers are always needed to transport foster kids for visitations with their parents, to school, child care, or medical appointments.

National Foster Parents Association
www.nfpainc.org
800-557-5238
7512 Stanich Avenue #6, Gig Harbor, WA 98335
This group is dedicated to supporting foster parents and providing information on foster care. (See "Frequently Asked Questions" on the website if you're considering becoming a foster family.)

Become a crisis shelter family. Volunteer to take a child into your home for a day or more to provide parents who are in crisis a break to sort out their lives. Contact your local Children's Home Society or crisis nursery for information on respite programs in your area.

Donate toys. Start a ritual in which you and your children go through their toys and books just before the holidays or a birthday. Decide which items they no longer play with, collect the ones that are in good condition, and then donate them to a hospital, shelter, or children's home.

Start a Care Bags for Kids program. Fill bags with fun and essential items for children in need. Contact the Care Bags Foundation for a starter kit.

Care Bags Foundation
www.carebags4kids.org

Help at a daycare center. Children can always use some extra attention. Your family can spend time with young children by assisting staff in planning and leading age-appropriate activities. Read books, play games, and make conversation with the kids. Call Head Start or your local YMCA.

Head Start
www2.acf.dhhs.gov/programs/hsb/
202-205-8572
800-763-6481
330 C Street, SW, Washington, DC 20447
This federal child development program serves low-income children between birth and age 5. Its goal is to increase school readiness. Check the website to find a program in your area. Then call your local Head Start and ask how your family can help.

BOX OF LOVE

Melissa Morrill and her 8-year-old son, Joey, of Yarmouth, Maine, spent one afternoon picking out party hats and plates, a cake mix, candles, and a gift to celebrate a sixth birthday in style. Then they packed the items in a box and mailed them to Mississippi. All for a boy they've never met. The Morrills are volunteers for the Box Project, a Connecticut-based organization that matches families in need of friendship and aid with those who want to help. The Morrills send their family one box each month filled with food, clothing, school supplies, or other essentials. Everyone in the family gets in on the act. Joey exchanges letters with the family's son, and his 19-year-old sister, Sarah, helps find items to include in the packages. "I told my kids that this family's not as lucky as us, they don't have as much money, and sometimes they can't buy stuff that they need," says Morrill. "It's definitely taught my kids not to be so greedy themselves." Now, on shopping trips, Morrill's 4-year-old daughter, Breanna, asks, "Do they need anything?" referring to their "box" family. For Melissa Morrill, though, it's more than a volunteer job. She and her Mississippi counterpart spend time sharing their lives through letters and phone calls: "She's a wonderful lady. I feel like we're friends."

☀ Join the Box Project. This organization matches sponsors with needy families in rural areas of the United States. The sponsoring family sends a box once per month filled with clothing, food, or other needed items and offers encouragement, friendship, and support.

Box Project
www.boxproject.org
800-268-9928
P.O. Box 435, Plainville, CT 06062

☀ Help refugee families. Provide friendship to refugees who are new to America. Loneliness is often a problem because relatives and friends are left behind in their home countries. These organizations may have resettlement programs for refugees in your area.

Association of Jewish Family and Children's Agencies
www.ajfca.org
800-634-7346

Catholic Charities
www.catholiccharitiesusa.org
703-549-1390

Church World Service
www.churchworldservice.org
800-297-1516

Lutheran Social Services in America
www.lutheranservices.org
800-664-3848

After you find a refugee family, here are some ways to help:

- Provide social contacts, listen to their stories, and take them on outings.

- Collect clothing or household items for the family.

- Introduce them to American customs and help them practice English. Learn some of their language, too.

- Assist with practical skills, such as making medical appointments, helping with a job search, registering children for school, or using public transportation.

- Greet the family at the airport when they arrive.

- Welcome a family into your home for their first weeks in the country until they find an apartment.

☼ Mentor an at-risk family. Provide help with résumé writing, budgeting, or other practical skills for a family struggling with poverty or other issues. Help the family cope with the demands of parenting. Maintain weekly contact. Your local Salvation Army may be able to help you find a family in need.

Salvation Army
www.salvationarmyusa.org
615 Slaters Lane, P.O. Box 269, Alexandria, VA 22313
This international organization serves the elderly, refugees, children, and people with disabilities.

☼ Assemble comfort kits: Some Red Cross affiliates collect Comfort Kits for children and adults affected by disasters. Place the following essential items in a resealable zipper bag:

ADULT COMFORT KIT:

toothpaste (.85 oz.), toothbrush and holder, soap (3.5 oz.) and washcloth, shampoo (8 oz.), comb (8"), tissues, deodorant (1.5 oz.), lotion (2 oz.), shaving cream (2oz.), and razor

CHILD COMFORT KIT:

soap (3.5 oz.) and washcloth, shampoo (8 oz.), comb (8"), toothpaste (.85 oz.), toothbrush and holder, pencil and sharpener, crayons, and writing pad

comfort kits

Call your local Red Cross for more information.

American Red Cross
www.redcross.org
202-303-4498
2025 E Street, NW, Washington, DC 20006

☼ Join the Poster Partner Program. The National Center for Missing and Exploited Children (NCMEC) will send you photos of missing children via the Internet. Your job is to print the photos and display them in your community to help locate these children.

National Center for Missing and Exploited Children
www.ncmec.org
703-274-3900; 800-THE-LOST (hotline)
699 Prince Street, Alexandria, VA 22314

☼ Help with a program that encourages inner city students to play soccer and learn creative writing. Your family can adopt a player or a team, help with special events or coaching in one of the eight cities where America Scores is located or start a new site.

America Scores
www.americascores.org
212-868-9510
520 Eighth Avenue, Suite 801, New York 10018

Ideas for "Crafty" Families

If you and your creative offspring love craft projects—why not direct some of that energy toward helping those in need? These are activities you and your children can do from home and on your own schedule.

☀ Knit, crochet, quilt, or sew. Make blankets, newborn caps, toecaps, lap robes, hats, mittens, or scarves for a variety of people and causes. Contact local hospitals, homeless shelters, or crisis nurseries to see what they need. The following organizations can provide instructions and suggestions.

> **ABC Quilts Home Office**
> **www.abcquilts.org**
> **800-536-5694**
> Offers specific quilting guidelines and ideas about where to donate the quilts.

> **Binky Patrol Comforting Covers for Kids**
> **www.binkypatrol.org**
> Your family can make "binkies" (homemade blankets) by sewing, knitting, crocheting, or quilting. Also, find a pattern for a simple "no sew" blanket children can make.

> **TLC for Angels**
> **www.tlcforangels.com**
> **732-886-0643**
> **850 Fort Plains Road, Howell, NJ 07731-1190**
> Handmade blankets, sweaters, booties, toys and more are donated to hospitals.

> **Warm Up America**
> **www.craftyarncouncil.com/warmup.html**
> Crochet or knit a rectangle (or more) and send it in where it will be joined with others to create a full-size afghan for someone in need.

> **The Warming Families Project**
> **www.warmingfamilies.org**
> Delivers blankets and other warm items to homeless families.

> For more organizations that provide crafts for charity, visit:

> **www.craftbits.com/html/crafts4charity.htm**
> **www.sewing.about.com/library/weekly/aa031798.htm**

☀ Put together activity boxes. Decorate a shoebox and fill it with activities for kids who are hospitalized and need fun ways to entertain themselves. Include a deck of cards, small games, activity books, and other items. Then distribute the boxes at a children's hospital.

> **Kid's Stuff USA**
> **Shoe Box Gifts**
> **www.feedthechildren.org** (click on **Kid's Stuff USA**)

☼ Make playdough. This inexpensive project is fun for kids of all ages. After it's made, donate the playdough to children in a hospital or homeless shelter. Or take it along when you visit kids who could use some amusement.

☼ Bake homemade treats. Many people would be heartened by a gift of homemade cookies, bars, or bread. Donate your baked goods to an elderly neighbor or a sick friend.

PLAYDOUGH RECIPE

3 ½ cups flour
1½ cups salt
3 cups water
6 teaspoons cream of tartar
3 tablespoons cooking oil
food coloring

Mix dry ingredients together. Mix wet ingredients together. Blend both batches, then stir over low heat until it forms a ball. Knead a bit, let cool. Store in a resealable zipper bag or plastic container.

recipe

☼ Make greeting cards. Every member of your family can create handmade cards. These can be "Get well soon" or simply "Thinking of you." Then you can walk from room to room in your local hospital or veteran's hospital and distribute them to patients or simply give them to the attending nurse to distribute.

Enchanted Learning
www.enchantedlearning.com/crafts
Click on "cards" for creative card-making possibilities.

Resources for Lending Support to Children and Families

Organizations and Websites

YMCA

www.ymca.net

The Y offers a variety of programs to support children and families. Call your local chapter to find out how your family can get involved.

YWCA
www.ywca.org

Contact your local YWCA for information on mentoring, after-school programs, and other volunteer possibilities.

Healing the Earth 4

We are stewards of an amazing planet. But are we doing our jobs? Take this quiz to find out.

True or False?

- ☼ We are losing forests at the rate of 10,000 acres a day. (False. The actual rate is closer to 100,000 acres per day.)

- ☼ Most people recycle their newspapers. (False. 88% of all newspapers are never recycled.)

- ☼ A million people each year die prematurely because of pollution. (False. Actually, the number is 3 million as a result of acute and chronic respiratory infections from air pollution and 2.2 million from contaminated water.)

- ☼ About 137 species become extinct every day. (True. And it's largely because of the encroachment of humans on their habitats.)

Are you surprised by the answers? Unfortunately, we're destroying habitats, polluting the air and water, filling the atmosphere with greenhouse emissions, and loading the landfills with garbage. Although the world is large and our families are small, we can play an effective role in healing the planet. You can help change the world each time you volunteer in a park or wildlife center, protect animals, or educate others about environmental hazards.

Support the Rights of Animals

We share our planet with 9 to 10 million species of animals, and we should treat them with compassion and respect. If you love animals, your family can volunteer to help any creature, great or small.

Ideas for Supporting the Rights of Animals

☼ Adopt an animal from your local animal shelter. If your family is looking for a pet, you might find it at your local humane society. The Humane Society offers guidelines for choosing the right animal for you and your kids. After you decide what type of animal will suit your family best, locate your local animal shelter (look in the phone book under "humane societies" or "animal shelters") and spend some time with the animals there to find the one you want.

The Humane Society of the United States
www.hsus.org
202-452-1100
2100 L Street, NW, Washington DC 20037
Find dozens of suggestions on how you can live your life in a way that reduces animal suffering.

☼ Assist at an animal shelter. Your family can clean and repair cages, play with and groom the animals, provide maintenance, or teach others about responsible pet ownership. Check the Yellow Pages under "animal shelters" or "humane societies." Be sure to check with your local humane society about age requirements for children who wish to volunteer.

TAKING CARE

Caring for animals has been a family affair at the Sylvestre household for five years. In addition to their own two cats and two dogs, the family fosters pets awaiting adoption—including pregnant animals, litters of puppies or kittens, or animals that need extra attention because of illness or neglect. The foster care coordinator at the humane society in Golden Valley, Minnesota calls when animals are available, and the Sylvestres decide whether their schedule permits them to take on a boarder (sometimes for a few weeks, other times for up to three months). While Alice Sylvestre is the primary caregiver, her husband, John, and her children (Anna, 21; Peter, 17; Marc, 14) are indispensable when it comes to socializing the animals. They often provide the play time each morning, afternoon, and evening that's required to get them adoption-ready. (And every animal the Sylvestres have cared for in the program has been adopted. Alice always checks.) A gentle home can take care of a lot of trauma, says Alice, and that's gratifying for the family. "It's good to know you can do a small thing and it makes a big difference."

volunteering

☼ Be a foster family to a pet awaiting adoption. Volunteer to care for abandoned dogs or cats, or animals that are pregnant, elderly, injured, or ill. Parrots and other birds awaiting adoption also need foster care. Sometimes families are asked to bring the pets to adoption fairs to help find them permanent homes. This volunteer job requires a lot of time, energy, and patience. Contact your local humane society for more information.

☼ Provide transportation for pets needing rescue or awaiting adoption. If you don't have the time to provide foster care, your family can help by being on call to transport animals to the vet, to adoption fairs, and for rescues.

☼ Work at adoption fairs for animals. People go to these fairs when they are looking for a pet. Individuals and humane societies bring animals awaiting adoption to the fairs. Your family can help with setup and cleanup, greet potential adopters, hold the pets on leashes, and make sure the animals have water. Check with your local animal shelter.

☼ Donate supplies to an animal shelter. Needed items might include pet food, toys, or bedding. Call your local shelter for ideas.

☼ Raise dogs for people with disabilities. Be part of a year-long program to raise and train a puppy to be a leader dog for a blind person. Canine Companions for Independence provides dogs for people with a variety of disabilities. You can be part of its puppy-raising program.

Leader Dogs for the Blind
www.leaderdog.org
248-650-7114 or 888-777-5332
P.O. Box 5000, Rochester, MI 48308

Canine Companions for Independence
www.caninecompanions.org
800-572-BARK (2275) will send your call to the nearest regional center.
866-CCI-DOGS (224-3647) is the number for the National Headquarters.
2965 Dutton Avenue, P.O. Box 446, Santa Rosa, CA 95402-0446

☼ Offer to walk dogs or provide other pet care for friends or neighbors who are elderly, disabled, or simply going out of town for a few days. Explain that you love animals and ask how your family can help.

☼ Work at a veterinary clinic or animal hospital. Here you can clean, feed, and care for animals, or prepare animals for surgery. Some members of your family might help with office work. Another way to help is by volunteering in a wildlife hospital. Your family can assist veterinarians, clean cages, and prepare food for injured wildlife. Be sure to ask about any age requirements for child volunteers.

☼ Work at a national wildlife refuge. There are 500 in the United States. Your family might help with projects or outreach, maintain trails and facilities, care for animals, or conduct research. To find out what's available in your area, visit http://refuges.fws.gov.

☼ Volunteer at a zoo or aquarium. This may or may not entail working directly with animals. Family volunteers might give tours, clean and feed animals, educate visitors, track animal behavior, do animal demonstrations, perform research and observation, or work at special events. To find a zoo or aquarium in your area, consult the American Zoo and Aquarium Association at www.aza.org or check the Yellow Pages under "zoos." Be sure to ask about any age requirements for child volunteers.

☼ Sponsor an animal. For $20 or more, your family can "adopt" a wild animal. Your money is used to protect the animals and their habitats through education, research, and conservation projects. You'll probably receive a photo of the animal, adoption papers or sponsorship certificate, and possibly a newsletter or magazine subscription. You can also sponsor a zoo animal. Call your local zoo for information.

American Cetacean Society
www.acsonline.org
310-548-6279
P.O. Box 1391, San Pedro, CA 90733-1391
This worldwide whale and dolphin conservation organization supports advocacy, education, and research for the protection of whales, porpoises, and dolphins.

Defenders of Wildlife National Headquarters
www.defenders.org
202-682-9400
1130 17th Street, NW, Washington, DC 20030
Sponsor a sea otter, dolphin, whale, bear, polar bear, wolf, or snowy owl.

The Dian Fossey Gorilla Fund
www.gorillafund.org
Founded by Dian Fossey in 1978, this organization promotes the conservation of mountain gorillas and their habitats through research, education, and protection programs.

Friends of the Ocean
www.friendsoftheocean.org
This organization offers sponsorships for whales, dolphins, and sea turtles.

Pacific Whale Foundation
www.pacificwhale.org
This foundation has opportunities to speak out for its conservation campaigns.

☼ Start a backyard wildlife habitat project. Make your backyard friendly to wildlife by providing food, water, and cover.

National Wildlife Federation (NWF)
www.nwf.org/backyardwildlifehabitat
800-822-9919 or 703-438-6000
11100 Wildlife Center Drive, Reston, VA 20190-5362
The NWF offers a series of nature magazines for children of all ages, instructions for creating a backyard habitat, and suggestions for taking action to support wildlife.

☼ Be a frogwatch volunteer. Collect information about the frog and toad populations in your neighborhood. Frogwatch USA uses the information to learn more about the diversity of frog and toad populations and to emphasize the importance of protecting wetland habitats.

Frogwatch U.S.A.
www.frogwatch.org
202-797-6891
Frogwatch USA Coordinator, National Wildlife Federation, 1406 16th Street, NW
Suite 501, Washington, DC 20036

☼ Raise a monkey as an aide to a person with a disability. This is an enormous commitment of time and energy for a family, but it can be extremely satisfying. This volunteer opportunity is not suitable for families with children under 10 or families in which both parents work full-time.

Monkey Helpers for the Disabled
www.helpinghandsmonkeys.org
617-787-4419
541 Cambridge Street, Boston, MA 02134

☼ If you live in a rural area, offer to help your local farm museum care for its animals. You may be asked to help feed animals, clean their pens, and organize special projects or lead tours.

☼ Rescue rabbits. Like other pets, domestic rabbits are abandoned or escape and need to be rescued to save them from disease, starvation, or predators. They are cared for in foster homes or shelters until adoptive families can be found. Your family can donate vegetables or hay, or foster or adopt a rabbit. Visit the House Rabbit Society to find out whom to contact in your area for volunteer information.

House Rabbit Society
www.rabbit.org

☼ Provide horseback riding experience for children with disabilities. Therapeutic horseback riding is used to help children with a variety of mental and physical disabilities. Volunteers might help care for the horses, lead and walk with horse and rider for support, or assist with other duties. (Most volunteers are over 14 years old.)

North American Riding for the Handicapped Association
www.narha.org
800-369-RIDE (7433)
P.O. Box 33150, Denver, CO 80233

☼ Help reduce pet overpopulation. Stray pets often acquire disease or are injured or killed, and large numbers of pets in shelters must be euthanized when no homes can be found. Over 47 million dogs and cats are born each year, and 15 million of them are euthanized because there are no homes for them. Here's what your family can do to help control the domestic pet population.

- Instead of purchasing animals at pet stores, adopt them from your local humane society or animal shelter.

- Promote low-cost or free spay and neutering programs by contacting local and state officials and expressing your concern.

- Volunteer to drive animals to and from veterinary hospitals to be spayed or neutered.

- Educate others about pet overpopulation and encourage them to spay or neuter their pets.

- Distribute information about spay/neuter hotlines that provide information about low-cost spay/neuter services.

  Friends of Animals Hotline
  800-321-PETS
  www.friendsofanimals.org

  Spay/USA Hotline
  800-248-SPAY
  www.spayUSA.org

☼ Help save endangered species. More animals than ever are disappearing as humankind encroaches on their habitats. (Current extinction rates are 1,000 times faster than what would be normal without our interference.) Sadly, over 50,000 species disappear every year. The animals listed on the next page are in danger of extinction, but they can still be saved. Do your part for animals in danger of becoming extinct by adopting an endangered species. Learn about a species that is in danger of extinction in your area. Find out what must be done to save it and create an action plan.

Some endangered animals:

African elephant	Grizzly bear	Rattlesnake
Bactrian camel	Koala	Red wolf
Blue whale	Komodo dragon	Sea turtle
Boa constrictor	Leopard	Sperm whale
Florida panther	Lynx	Yak
Gorilla	Manatee	Zebra
Grey wolf	Orangutan	
Great white shark	Panda	

For a more complete list, contact the World Wildlife Fund at www.worldwildlife.org.

EXTINCTION: WHY IT HAPPENS, WHAT YOU CAN DO

**Ways humans contribute
to species extinction:**

- Use animals for food and clothing.
- Kill animals from carelessness or for profit.
- Contribute to pollution (dirty water, garbage, acid rain) and climate change.
- Take over animal habitats with our cities, roads, farms, and factories.
- Introduce animals into new areas, which may contribute to the destruction of existing wildlife in that location.
- Pass on human diseases to animals.

Ways to help:

- Don't dump trash or garbage in the water or on land.
- Take part in a clean-up project.
- Don't keep wild animals as pets.
- Don't buy products from endangered species, including fur, ivory, and coral.
- Advocate for biodiversity.
- Buy organic fruits and vegetable grown without pesticides, which may be harmful to animals.
- Learn about 101 things you can do to save animals from extinction. Visit:www.oregonzoo. org/ConservationResearch/ whatyou.htm

Be an animal activist. Take a stand for animal rights. (See Chapter 7 for tips on fighting for a cause.)

- Write letters or make calls to companies that use animals for cosmetic testing and let them know you will boycott their products.

- Support companies that are animal friendly.

- Lobby for animal welfare. Contact the American Association for the Prevention of Cruelty to Animals (ASPCA) and the Humane Society for information on animal rights issues. Respond to the action alerts on the websites.

ASPCA
www.aspca.org
212-876-7700
424 E. 92nd Street, New York, NY 10128
An organization dedicated to the welfare of animals through education and advocacy. The website provides a list of animal shelters by community. Or click and join the "ASPCA Advocacy Brigade" and receive periodic e-mails detailing how you can advocate for animal welfare.

- The Audubon Society encourages you to be an armchair activist for birds by writing one letter per month to lawmakers on issues related to bird protection.

National Audubon Society
www.audubon.org
212-979-3000
700 Broadway, New York, NY 10003

Resources for Supporting the Rights of Animals

Books for Kids

Can We Save Them? by David Dobson, illustrated by James M. Needham (Watertown, MA: Charlesbridge Publishing, 1997). Ages 4-8. A look at 12 North American species (including peregrine falcons, Peary caribou, and Puerto Rican parrots) threatened with extinction. Kids learn how humans have contributed to species extinction and what we can do to remedy it.

One Day at Wood Green Animal Shelter by Patricia Casey (Cambridge, MA: Candlewick Press, 2001). Ages 4-8. Learn about the workings of a humane society from this informative and lively book. Perfect for young animal lovers.

One Less Fish by Kim Michelle Toft and Allan Sheather (Watertown, MA: Charlesbridge Publishing, 1998). Ages 4-8. Every page features stunning silk-painted tropical fish and a reverse counting rhyme that describes why these colorful creatures are disappearing one by one. Discover the perils of offshore oil drilling and plastic bags in this beautiful and informative book.

And Then There Was One: The Mysteries of Extinction by Margery Facklam, illustrated by Pamela Johnson (Boston: Little, Brown, and Company, 1993). Ages 9-12. Examines extinction from both natural and human causes and discusses what can be done to save species.

How to Be Animal Friendly: Choose the Kindest Ways to Eat, Shop, and Have Fun by Philippa Perry and Caroline Grimshaw (New York: HarperCollins, 1999). Ages 9-12. Informs and inspires children to support the rights of animals, and includes information on extinction, factory farming, and animal testing.

Animal Rights by Jennifer Hurley (San Diego: Greenhaven Press, 1998). Young adult. This is in the series called "Opposing Viewpoints Digest." It presents arguments on both sides of animal rights issues, such as "Is Animal Experimentation Justified?"

Animal Rights: A Handbook for Young Adults by Daniel Cohen (Brookfield, CT: Millbrook Press, 1993). Young adult. Cohen informs teens about animal rights issues and advises them on how to make a difference. Readers learn the arguments for and against using animals for medical research, entertainment, and food and fur.

Working With Wildlife: A Guide to Careers in the Animal World by Thane Maynard (New York: Franklin Watts, 2000). Young adult. A practical guide for teens interested in working with animals. Readers learn about the work and training required to be a vet, field researcher, nature guide, conservationist, and dozens of other animal-related jobs.

Organizations and Websites

International Wildlife Rehabilitation Council
www.iwrc-online.org
A section of the website called "Camp Cottontail" introduces kids to wildlife.

People for the Ethical Treatment of Animals (PETA)
www.peta.org
757-622-7382
501 Front Street, Norfolk, VA 23510
Learn to eat vegetarian, order fact sheets on animal rights issues, and get up-to-date news from this high-profile animal rights group. The website has a special section for kids, including information on ending the practice of dissection in schools.

World Wildlife Fund
www.worldwildlife.org
202-293-4800
1250 24th Street, NW, Washington, DC 20037
Join the Action Network and receive e-mail updates on critical issues. The website includes a kid's section with interactive games, quizzes, and projects to help children learn about the wild animals and biodiversity.

Youth Corps for Animals
www.youthforanimals.org
This online resource connects children with volunteer opportunities with animals and animal rights groups and explains how to be an animal activist.

Preserve Parks and Wilderness Areas

Preserving wilderness areas is critical so that plants and animals can flourish in their natural habitats. According to the Sierra Club, the United States has already lost 95% of its old-growth forests and 90% of its prairies. We must take care of and maintain the spaces that are left both for us and for the generations to come. Helping to accomplish this can be fun, especially for families who love the outdoors.

Ideas for Preserving Parks and Wilderness Areas

☼ Work for your state's Department of Natural Resources (DNR). The DNR's mission is to protect the environment, and it depends on volunteers to help. Projects might include removing non-native plants, building fencing, and reseeding or transplanting trees or shrubs. Groups are often welcome, so get several families together to work. Contact your state's DNR for information on specific volunteer opportunities for families.

☼ Organize a fundraiser to help save the rainforest (see Chapter 7 for ideas on fundraising).

WHY SAVE THE RAINFORESTS?

Rainforests are home to a huge variety of plants, animals, and insects. In fact, between 50% and 70% of all known species reside there. And many of them benefit humankind. For example, one-quarter of all medicines are derived from rainforest plants. In addition, more than 1,000 indigenous tribes depend on the rainforest for food, shelter, medicine, clothing, and clean water. As this land disappears, these people will lose their culture and traditions, animal and plant species will die out (they're disappearing at the rate of 137 per day), and we will no longer have access to the rainforest's valuable resources. Do your part to protect them. Don't buy rare plants, woods, or animals taken from the rainforest. Cut down on your use of paper, plastic, and gasoline. Eat less red meat. And, consider joining a rainforest protection group.

facts

☼ Retrieve trash from local rivers, lakes, or streams. Spend a few hours cleaning up a local waterway with your family or several families. You can also get involved with an organization that is working to save local rivers. Contact River Network to find out what's happening in your area.

River Network
National Office
www.rivernetwork.org
800-423-6747 or 503-241-3506
520 SW 6th Avenue, #1130, Portland, OR 97204

☼ Organize an event for National Parks week. A booklet available from the National Park Service will help you plan a March for Parks. If your community already sponsors a march, join in!

National Park Service
www.nps.gov/npweek/march.htm
202-354-2182
Partnership Office #2206
1849 C Street, NW, Washington, DC 20240

☼ Help transform an old railroad line into a trail. All over the country, former rail lines are being converted into trails for cycling, in-line skating, hiking, cross-country skiing, and running.

Rails-to-Trails Conservancy
www.railtrails.org
202-331-9696
1100 17th Street, NW, Washington, DC 20036

☼ Volunteer with your local parks department. You could clear trails, work in a visitor's center, collect fees, garden, or help with landscape maintenance and cleanup. You can find the phone number of your local parks department in the blue pages of the phone book.

☼ Volunteer at a nature center. Families may staff the center, conduct interpretive programs, and assist with trail maintenance and patrol.

☼ Adopt a park. Inspect a local park on a regular basis, pick up litter, and look for problems.

☼ Adopt an area of your neighborhood that needs loving care. Clean it, plant trees, and install a bird feeder. Get permission from local authorities if the area is city property. If it's privately owned, ask if your family or neighborhood group can help beautify it.

☼ Start a neighborhood yard waste composting site. Instead of throwing away organic waste (grass clippings, leaves, kitchen scraps), help your neighbors learn how to compost it. Find a spot accessible to everyone who is interested. Not only will you be saving the landfills, but you'll also produce free organic fertilizer.

☀ **Push for more public land.** We need open spaces. Your family can make it happen by lobbying your city council to expand the park system. For more information, contact the Trust for Public Land (TPL).

TPL National Office
www.tpl.org
415-495-4014
116 New Montgomery Street, 4th Floor, San Francisco, CA 94105

☀ **Plant a tree.** We need trees to maintain the balance of carbon dioxide and oxygen in the air. And they're beautiful besides. Contact the National Arbor Day Foundation for low-cost trees and directions for planting. Or check out the Treemusketeers website for lots of tree information for kids and their adult friends.

National Arbor Day Foundation
www.arborday.org
100 Arbor Avenue, Nebraska City, NE 68410
For a $10 membership fee, you'll receive 10 flowering trees or Colorado Blue Spruces to plant.

Treemusketeers
www.treemusketeers.org
310-322-0263
136 Main Street, Suite A, El Segundo, CA 90245

Resources for Preserving Parks and Wilderness Areas

Books for Children

Where Once There Was a Wood by Denise Fleming (New York: Henry Holt and Company, 2000). Ages 3-6. Simple rhyming text explains the natural world that existed before houses and neighborhoods were built. Added notes for parents and older children explain how to establish a backyard habitat.

The Forest Has Eyes by Elise MacLay, illustrated by Bev Doolittle (Shelton, CT: Greenwich Workshop Press, 1998). Ages 4-8. Have fun with this lushly drawn "camouflage art," with pictures hidden within. Learn about Native American culture and their reverence for the land and the animals that inhabit the forests.

Everglades by Jean Craighead George, paintings by Wendell Minor (New York: HarperCollins, 1999). Ages 5-10. A storyteller describes the Florida Everglades as she guides children through this one-of-a-kind ecosystem. Minor's paintings depict the beauty of this home to alligators and egrets.

Ancient Ones: The World of the Old-Growth Douglas Fir by Barbara Bash (San Francisco: Sierra Club Books for Children, 2002). Ages 8-11. The majesty of the forest is captured in the text and watercolor paintings.

The Complete Backyard Nature Activity Book: Fun Projects for Kids to Learn About the Wonders of Wildlife and Nature by Robin Michal Koontz (New York: Learning Triangle Press, 1998). Ages 8-12. Kids can learn about creating habitats in their own backyards for butterflies, frogs, hummingbirds, and more.

How Monkeys Make Chocolate: Foods and Medicines From the Rainforests by Adrian Forsyth (Toronto: Owl Communications, 1995). Ages 9-12. Get lots of information about the plants, animals, and people of the rainforest and their intricate web of interdependence.

The Most Beautiful Roof in the World: Exploring the Rainforest Canopy by Kathryn Lasky, photographs by Christopher G. Knight (San Diego: Harcourt, Brace & Company, 1997). Ages 9-12. Enter the world of the rainforest canopy with Meg Lowman, a scientist who is exploring this home to thousands of species of plants and animals.

Hatchet by Gary Paulsen (New York: Simon and Schuster, 1999). Young adult. The award-winning story of 13-year-old Brian Robeson's struggle to survive after a plane crash in the Canadian wilderness. A classic.

Julie of the Wolves by Jean Craighead George (New York: HarperCollins, 1987). Young adult. A young Eskimo girl gets lost in the Alaskan tundra after running away to find her San Francisco pen pal and is taken in by a pack of Arctic wolves. This Newberry Award winner is a tale of survival and much more.

Organizations

American Forestry Association, Global Releaf Program
www.americanforests.org
202-955-4500
P.O. Box 2000, Washington, DC 20013
Learn why trees are so important and how you can help bring "releaf" to the planet. For every dollar you donate, this group will plant a tree.

Conservation International (CI)
www.conservation.org
Toll-free: 800-406-2306
202-912-1000
1919 M Street, NW, Suite 600, Washington, DC 20036

Dedicated to preserving the earth's biodiversity, CI focuses on "hotspots," the small percentage of the earth's land with the richest collection of plant and animal species.

The Nature Conservancy
www.nature.org
Membership: 800-628-6860
Worldwide Office: 703-841-5300
4245 North Fairfax Drive, Suite 100, Arlington, VA 22203-1606

By visiting the website or calling the Nature Conservancy, you can find the chapter in your state and discover what volunteering opportunities are available. You can also join the Adopt-an-Acre program for $75.

The Rainforest Action Network's Kids Corner
www.ran.org/kids_action

You'll find rainforest crafts, activities, fact sheets, movies, and ways to help.

Rainforest Alliance
www.rainforest-alliance.org
888-MY-EARTH or 212-677-1900
665 Broadway, Suite 500, New York, NY 10012

Find lots of information on conservation issues, activities for kids, rainforest-friendly products, and ideas for getting involved.

Sierra Club
www.sierraclub.org
415-977-5500
85 Second Street, Second Floor, San Francisco, CA 94105

Learn about a variety of environmental concerns, from global warming to responsible trade. Find out how you can take action on timely issues.

Join Cleanup and Recycling Efforts

What's in your garbage? Probably just about everything—moldy leftovers, corroded batteries, out-of-date magazines, plastic detergent bottles, and old toilet paper rolls. On average, we throw away 4.4 pounds of garbage per person each day—almost twice as much as people in other major countries. It really adds up. According to the Environmental Defense Fund, the paper we throw away annually could build a wall 12 feet high stretching from Los Angeles to New York City. And we toss enough aluminum in the trash to rebuild our entire commercial air fleet every three months. Unfortunately, fewer locations are available for landfills than before and they are expensive to maintain. Your family can support recycling efforts as well as educate others about how to produce less garbage.

Ideas for Joining Cleanup and Recycling Efforts

☼ Clean up litter. Take a section of park, beach, or vacant lot and clear it of litter. Your family can do this on your own or become part of a clean-up team. (Read the safety tips below before you begin.) This can be a one-time project or a regular event. Organize your neighbors to lend a hand.

SAFETY TIPS FOR CLEANUPS

Here are some suggestions for making sure your cleanup is safe for everyone involved:

1. Wear sturdy gloves.
2. Be careful of snakes, stinging insects, poisonous plants, and stray animals.
3. Be careful handling sharp objects.
4. Certain objects, such as broken glass, should be handled by adults only.
5. Wear long pants, sunscreen, and insect repellent.
6. Wash hands afterwards.
7. Supervise children closely. (Most adopt-a-highway programs do not allow children under 12 years to take part in the project.)
8. Wear safety vests if you're cleaning up near a road.
9. Don't pick up discarded hypodermic needles, syringes, chemicals, or other hazardous materials. If you're suspicious, don't touch it.
10. Don't pack trash bags too full. (Stuffing them may cause injuries from jagged objects.)
11. Don't work after dusk.
12. Take breaks and drink plenty of fluids.
13. Stay alert to any nearby traffic.
14. Be careful on the banks of creeks or rivers that may be slippery.

☼ Adopt a monument. Care for it. Keep it clean and keep the weeds away.

☼ Participate in the Adopt-a-Highway program. Remove litter and in some cases plant seedling trees and wildflowers. Contact your state's Department of Transportation for more information about how your family can get involved.

- ☼ Work at a recycling plant. This may involve sorting recyclables, helping with drop-offs, or cleaning. To find a recycling plant in your area, check the Yellow Pages under "Recycling Services."

- ☼ Have a recycling drive. This is a great way to reduce waste and raise money for a worthy cause. (Often, recycled materials can be sold to manufacturers). Organize your neighborhood, school, or church to collect aluminum cans. Then deliver them to the local recycling center.

- ☼ Conduct a recycling awareness campaign. Urge your community to increase recycling rates by letting others know the benefits of recycling. Write letters to the editor, make posters, pass petitions, and talk to neighbors and friends.

- ☼ Establish recycling containers. Have you noticed the lack of recycling containers in a local park, community center, or school? Help remedy the situation by advocating to have containers donated.

- ☼ Buy and decorate reusable shopping bags for family and friends. Help others stop wasting paper and plastic by donating attractive cloth shopping bags that can be used again and again.

HIGHWAY HELPERS

Sometimes as many as 30 adults and children show up to clean the strip of Highway 81 adopted by the local 4H Club of Sedgwick County, Kansas. Jeff and Shelley Colborn, the group's leaders, along with their children, Josh, 17, and Shelby, 16, meet other 4Hers (and some of their parents) twice each year at the nearby Peck Community Center. The children who are too young to pick up litter near a busy highway stay to clean up trash at the center. The others head out to fill trash bags with pop bottles, cigarettes, and beer cans left by careless passersby. "There are so few people who feel a tie to their community anymore, and because of that, the kids don't take care of it," says Shelley Colborn. "But through this kind of service my kids have learned the value of community and want to do their part to make it a better place."

volunteering

Resources for Cleanup and Recycling Efforts

Books for Kids

Where the Garbage Goes, a video by Fred Levine Productions, 1997. Ages 3-8. Kids can learn about garbage and recycling while watching lots of heavy equipment, such as grinders, loaders, and haulers, do its job.

Recycle That by Fay Robinson (Chicago: Children's Press, 1995). Ages 4-8. Simple explanation of recycling with photographs.

50 Simple Things Kids Can Do to Recycle by the Earth Works Group, illustrated by Michele Montez (Berkeley, CA: EarthWorks Press, 1994). Ages 9-12. Recycle at home, at school and in your community. This book will tell you how.

Waste Disposal by Sally Morgan (New York: Franklin Watts, 2000). Ages 8-12. Find out where waste (nuclear, dirty water, garbage, toxic) goes and how it affects the environment. Also learn about recycling metals, glass, and paper, and discover what kids can do to help deal with waste.

Garbage and Recycling: Opposing Viewpoints edited by Helen Cothran (San Diego: Greenhaven Press, 2003). Young adult. Provides varying points of view on whether garbage and toxic waste are serious problems, the effectiveness of recycling, and the innovations that will reduce waste.

Organizations and Websites

Learner.org
www.learner.org/exhibits/garbage
Learn about garbage, hazardous waste, and sewage and find out what your community can do to reduce waste.

Recycle City
www.epa.gov/recyclecity/
Games, activities, and stories to help kids learn about reducing waste and encouraging recycling.

National Recycling Coalition
www.nrc-recycle.org
202-347-0450
1325 G Street, NW, Suite 1025, Washington, DC 20005
Find out what's happening on America Recycles Day and learn how you can become involved.

Web Directory—Recycling
www.webdirectory.com/recycling
Find links to everything you want to know about recycling.

Become Environmental Educators and Activists

Do you think disposable diapers are the greatest source of garbage for our nation's landfills? Lots of people do, but actually paper is the biggest landfill problem. According to a 1998 survey by the National Environmental Education and Training Foundation, most Americans can't separate environmental myths from environmental facts. Some other misconceptions: A majority of Americans believe that most of our power is generated by non-polluting sources (it's not), and are unaware that the primary source of oil pollution is improperly disposed of car oil. Also, the leading cause of childhood death globally is microorganisms in water (i.e., water pollution), not famine, as most Americans believe. Educating ourselves and others about the environment is a critical first step in healing our planet. Your family can be active and informed environmentalists.

Ideas to Support Environmental Education and Activism

☼ Become environmental activists.

- Stage a boycott. Has your family discovered products that are a danger to the environment? Boycott that product and encourage those you know to do the same. Write a letter to the company explaining your reasons for the boycott.

- Write a letter to the editor about your environmental concerns. Focus on a recent news item or story.

- Elect candidates friendly to the environment. For more information on what your family can do to elect the candidate of your choice, see Chapter 7.

- Lobby for environmental issues. Go door to door asking for support, getting a petition signed, or soliciting financial contributions for an organization or issue. Meet with your local, state, or national representatives to explain why they should support the environmental issue you're advocating.

- The Sierra Club provides a sitelet called "Take Action" for information on such issues as global warming, energy, population, and responsible trade. There is also an "activists toolkit" with information on why and how to make a difference, including tips on letter writing.

  The Sierra Club
  www.sierraclub.org
  415-977-5500
  85 Second Street, Second Floor, San Francisco, CA 94105

● The Environmental Defense Fund has an online action center where you can make your voice heard on timely environmental issues.

Environmental Defense Fund
www.edf.org
800-684-3322
257 Park Avenue South, New York, NY 10010
Stay informed with up-to-date information on environmental concerns and "action alerts" that tell you whom to write or call to make your voice heard.

☼ Celebrate Earth Day. The first Earth Day, on April 22, 1970, in many ways marked the beginning of the modern environmental movement. This is an ideal time to reflect on what ails our planet and how we can repair it. There's a lot your family can do to celebrate Earth Day and raise awareness of the serious environmental issues facing our planet.

● Create an awareness campaign at your child's school. Earth Day is all about education. Do your part by helping children understand environmental issues and how they can make a difference.

● Organize a community festival. More than 100 are held around the country each year on Earth Day. Make your town one of them.

● Plant trees, pick up litter, organize a letter-writing campaign or fundraising walk for environmental causes, or take part in any other activity that helps make a difference for our planet.

To get dozens of ideas for what your family can do on Earth Day or to find out what's happening in your community, visit these websites:

Earth Day Network
www.earthday.net

Earth Day Event Ideas
http://earthday.envirolink.org/guide6.html

☼ Share facts about the environment with school groups, other families, and your community. Your family might offer to teach a community education class, an after-school class, or hold a community meeting about environmental issues.

☼ Organize an environmental fair at school. You could invite environmental groups to give presentations. Include games and exhibits. Students can create projects and local businesses might donate prizes for the best ones.

☼ Volunteer at an environmental learning or nature center. Your family might help maintain the grounds, assist educators, conduct tours, or coordinate fundraisers.

☼ Join an environmental group. There are lots of ways your family can help organizations dedicated to the environment. Call and ask how you might contribute. Some possibilities include:

● Go door to door to raise money or pass out literature.

● Attend meetings.

● Educate others about your group's mission.

● Organize campaigns or fundraisers.

Resources for Supporting Environmental Awareness

Books for Kids

Our Big Home: An Earth Poem by Linda Glaser, illustrated by Elisa Kleven (Brookfield, CT: The Millbrook Press, 2002). Ages 4-8. An inspirational poem, along with whimsical drawings about what everyone on the planet shares—water, sky, and sun.

Dinosaurs to the Rescue: A Guide to Protecting Our Planet by Laury Krasny Brown and Marc Brown (Boston: Little Brown & Co., 1994). Ages 4-8. Cartoon characters teach kids all the ways they can help save the earth, from collecting trash for recycling to using less water and electricity.

The Lorax by Dr. Seuss (New York: Random House, 1976). Ages 4-8. A rhyming account of an ecological crisis in the Truffula forest. A video is also available.

50 Simple Things Kids Can Do to Save the Earth by The EarthWorks Group, illustrated by Michele Montez (Kansas City: Andrew McMeel Publishing, 1990). Ages 5-12. A series of practical ideas for what kids can do to heal the planet. Lots of fun facts and clear explanations.

Ecology by Steve Pollock (London: DK Publishing, Inc., 2000). Ages 9-12. An Eyewitness Science book filled with information, photos, and drawings that teach about food webs, the water cycle, ecological niches, population growth, and evolution.

Hoot by Carl Hiaasen (New York: Knopf Publishing, 2002). Ages 9-12. An ecological mystery for middle schoolers in which Roy, a new kid at school, sets out to save some burrowing owls from developers.

How to Save the Planet by Barbara Taylor, illustrated by Scoular Anderson (New York: Franklin Watts, 2001). Ages 9-12. Fun, simple, and comprehensive source for explanations of important environmental issues, including ozone depletion, pollution, garbage, and habitat extinction.

The Complete Guide to Environmental Careers in the 21st Century by the Environmental Careers Organization (Washington, D.C.: Island Press, 1999). Young adult and adult. If you or one of your teens are considering an environmentally-related career, check out dozens of possibilities in this comprehensive guide.

Dr. Art's Guide to Planet Earth: For Earthlings Ages 12 to 120 by Art Sussman, Ph.D., illustrated by Emiko Koike (San Francisco: WestEd Publishing, 2000). Young adult. A systems approach to how the earth works that is compelling, well-organized, and understandable. There are also recommendations for what young people can do to help save the planet.

Organizations

Amazing Environmental Web Directory
www.webdirectory.com

"The earth's biggest environment search engine."

Childsake
www.childsake.com

Products and children's books related to animals, nature, and environmental issues. The book list is comprehensive, and all books are reviewed.

Eco-Kids
www.ecokidsonline.com

Activities, games, stories, and art that gets kids interested in and informed about environmental issues.

Kids for a Clean Environment
www.kidsface.org
615-331-7381
P.O. Box 158254, Nashville, TN 37215

A run-by-kids organization whose latest mission, called Earth Odyssey, focuses on land conservation through recycling, habitat protection, and air quality. Kids can get information on environmental issues or start their own chapter.

U.S. Environmental Protection Agency
www.epa.gov

Click on "Explorer's Club for Kids" to learn about pollution and other environmental issues.

Reference

1998 NEETF/Roper Report Card: Environmental Myths in America: An Average American View can be ordered from the National Environmental Education & Training Foundation (NEETF) at www.neetf.org.

Fighting Poverty 5

Imagine seeing your children hungry, cold, or sick and being unable to provide for them. That's a reality for the nearly one in five kids living below the poverty line in this country. Worldwide, the problem is much worse. According to Bread for the World, a hunger relief organization (www.bread.org), about one-fifth of the planet's population (1.2 billion people) survives on less than $1 a day, and 840 million people are malnourished. As individuals, we can make an impact on the devastating poverty that plagues so much of the world.

If your family is concerned about people in poverty, begin by educating yourself and your children about the causes of poverty and ways to help. Then go to work. From promoting awareness of homelessness to packing groceries for a food bank, each of us can do our part to ensure that every person receives the basic necessities of life.

Get Food to the Hungry

In 2002, the U.S. Department of Agriculture reported that 11 million U.S. households were "food insecure," meaning they were hungry or living on the edge of hunger. In 3.3 million of those households, the problem was particularly severe. The physical and emotional suffering caused by hunger is not the only concern. When people—especially children—are inadequately nourished, the result is often poor health, developmental delays, and educational underachievement. Hungry children have difficulty in school, develop more slowly physically and mentally, and have trouble coping in their surroundings. Even the simple act of getting along with others becomes more difficult (www.chattfoodbank.org/kids%20cafe.htm). According to the Food Research and Action Center (FRAC) "While starvation seldom occurs in this country, children and adults do go hungry and chronic mild under-nutrition does occur when financial resources are low. The mental and physical changes that accompany inadequate food intakes can have harmful effects on learning, development, productivity, physical and psychological health, and family life" (www.frac.org/html/hunger_in_the_us/hunger_index.html). Here are some ways you can help.

Ideas for Getting Food to the Hungry

☀ Take part in National Hunger Awareness Day each year. America's Second Harvest created this event to raise awareness of hunger in America. Even small gestures make a difference: "For instance, for every one dollar donated, America's Second Harvest is able to distribute 28 pounds of food to hungry Americans and in just one hour of volunteer time you could sort more than 200 pounds of surplus food that ends up on the tables of hungry Americans."

America's Second Harvest
www.secondharvest.org
800-771-2303
35 E. Wacker Drive, #2000, Chicago, IL 60601

☀ Work at a food bank. Unload, pack food bags, sort, shelve, and distribute food. There may also be a need for office work and help with special events. To find the food bank or soup kitchen nearest you, contact America's Second Harvest (see above for complete contact information).

www.secondharvest.org

☀ Help prepare and serve food at a local Kids Café program. These are places where hungry kids can find hot meals. Kids Cafés also provide recreational and educational activities. There are more than 600 Kids Cafés nationwide. To locate the Kids Café nearest you, visit America's Second Harvest (see above for complete contact information).

www.secondharvest.org/childhunger/kidscafe.html

☀ Volunteer for the Women, Infant and Children (WIC) program, which serves pregnant and nursing women and children up to age 5 who are nutritionally at risk. This government program provides supplemental food, nutrition screening, and referrals to other social services. Your family might read and play with the children whose families are being served, help with administrative tasks, or assist in preparing educational information.

Food and Nutrition Service
www.fns.usda.gov/wic/
This website can help you find the WIC agency in your state.

☀ Volunteer to cook at a soup kitchen or homeless shelter. This is an activity ideally suited to an entire family or even several families together. Plan a simple meal that can be easily prepared for large numbers, such as spaghetti, tacos, or lasagna. Younger family members can set the table (or make table decorations) while older children and adults do the cooking. In addition, many shelters need people to make lunches. Usually shelters serve one or two hot meals a day. That may leave some residents with no option for a midday meal. Your family can volunteer to pack sandwiches for the shelter guests to eat during the day, or bake cookies, pies, or cakes for shelter residents who rarely get the treat of homemade food. Surprise them with a family specialty.

Donate food to a food bank. There are lots of ways to collect food to contribute, and many of them take little time. Make a trip to a discount store for nonperishable food, diapers, toilet articles, and cleaning supplies. Then drop them at your local food bank.

FACTS ABOUT HUNGER

statistics

- There is enough food worldwide to feed everybody. But not everybody can afford the food that's available. (Rehydration Project)
- In 1999, approximately 12 million American children were food insecure, meaning they were hungry or at risk of hunger. (Second Harvest)
- Recent research indicates that even mild under-nutrition experienced by young children during critical periods of growth may affect physical growth and brain development. (Second Harvest)
- In 2000, 62% of all requests for emergency food in American cities came from either children or their parents. (Second Harvest)
- One in five people in a soup kitchen line is a child. (Second Harvest)
- Each child in the industrialized world will consume 20 to 40 times as much as a child in a developing country in his or her lifetime. (Rehydration Project)
- 31 million Americans live in households that experience hunger or the risk of hunger. This represents one in 10 households in the United States. Children account for nearly 40% of this group. (Bread for the World)
- If all 31 million Americans faced with food insecurity stood in line at a food bank in New York City, the line would stretch to Los Angeles and back. Twice. (Share our Strength)
- Almost 70% of households at risk of hunger have someone who's employed, and 57% of at-risk households have at least one full-time worker. (Community Childhood Hunger Identification Project, 1995)

Make it a monthly ritual. Another idea is to choose one item each time your family goes to the grocery store. When you get a bagful, take it to the nearest food bank. Or, at your next family party, have each guest bring a food item to donate.

☼ Organize your church, civic organization, Scout troop, neighborhood, or school to conduct a food drive. Take your collection to a local food bank. Or, ask your local grocery store if your family can spend a Saturday afternoon sponsoring a food drive. Ask each shopper to buy an extra item to donate and place a bin in the store to collect food donations. Volunteer to empty the bin and deliver the donations to the food bank.

☼ Coordinate a food drive in conjunction with a school event. Every child who donates a food item receives a discounted ticket to the event.

☼ Deliver food from a food bank to the homebound. The elderly and those with disabilities have difficulty getting to a food bank. Call to see if your family can volunteer to bring food to the homebound, or start a delivery program if none exists. To find the food bank or soup kitchen nearest you, call America's Second Harvest (see page 82 for complete information).

America's Second Harvest
www.secondharvest.org

DELIVERING SMILES

Back in 1976, the Metropolitan Inter-faith Association (MIFA) in Memphis began delivering meals to the homebound. The Spence family volunteered to help out. They've been at it ever since. During these intervening years, members of five generations of the family at one time or another have spent their Thursday lunch hour at the task. Gayle Spence, her mother, and her four-year-old daughter made up the initial team. Then, when Spence's 98-year-old grandfather moved in with her mother, he began coming along. As Gayle had more children—six in all—some of them volunteered. Now, 26 years later, several of Spence's young grandchildren have become meal deliverers. Each Thursday, certain family members spend a couple hours together, handing out meals and visiting with the homebound people they serve. And after finishing their route, they all go out to lunch. "I think it's been a good experience for all of us to share with people from such diverse backgrounds and to realize that we all have wonderful gifts to contribute," says Spence.

volunteering

☼ Volunteer for your local Meals on Wheels program. Volunteer once a week or once a month. It usually takes about two hours, either at lunch or dinnertime.

Meals on Wheels Association of America
www.projectmeal.org
703-548-5558
1414 W. Prince Street, Suite 302, Alexandria, VA 22314
Click on "program links" to find a program in your community.

☼ Volunteer to glean. Up to one-fifth of food in the United States goes to waste. (That's an astounding 130 pounds per person.) The term gleaning (also called food rescue or food recovery) can include field gleaning (gathering crops left in the field after harvest or crops that were not profitable to harvest), perishable food rescue, nonperishable food collection, and the rescue of prepared foods. Not all food coming in to a food recovery organization is ready to be distributed, so volunteers are needed to repack it. Your family can also help with pick-up and delivery. Visit America's Second Harvest website or contact the National Hunger Clearinghouse for more information.

America's Second Harvest
www.secondharvest.org

National Hunger Clearinghouse
www.worldhungeryear.org/nhc
Hotline: 800-GLEAN-IT
Call to find out about food pantries and food recovery programs near you, how you can volunteer, and how to start a gleaning project. Read "A Citizen's Guide to Food Recovery," a USDA publication with a section on how individual citizens can help recover food.

United States Department of Agriculture
www.usda.gov/news/pubs/gleaning/content.htm

Society of St. Andrew
www.endhunger.org
800-333-4597 or 434-299-5956
3383 Sweet Hollow Road, Big Island, VA 24526
A Christian ministry that delivers food and services to the hungry through gleaning.

☼ Grow extra vegetables. Does your family have a vegetable garden? Grow some extra this year and donate the goods to your local food bank for immediate distribution.

Garden Writers Association
Plant a Row for the Hungry
www.gwaa.org/par/

☼ Give out fast food gift certificates to the homeless and hungry. Some people worry that if they give out money to the homeless and hungry, their dollars will be used for drugs and alcohol rather than food. Solve this problem by having family members purchase and carry certificates for fast food restaurants or a nearby grocery store to distribute to those in need.

Resources for Getting Food to the Hungry

Books for Kids

Uncle Willie and the Soup Kitchen by DyAnne DiSalvo-Ryan (New York: William Morrow and Co., 1997). Ages 6-8. Uncle Willy brings his nephew with him when he works at a soup kitchen.

Famine: The World Reacts by Paul Bennett (Mankato, MN: Smart Apple Media, 1999). Ages 9-12. Learn about the history of food shortages, why they occur, and what you can do to help.

Gracie's Girl by Ellen Wittlinger (New York: Simon and Schuster, 2000). Ages 9-12. Helping out at a soup kitchen doesn't seem "cool" to Bess, until she meets someone who puts a face on hunger and homelessness.

Food: The Struggle to Sustain the Human Community by Jake Goldberg (New York: Franklin Watts, 1999). Young adult and adult. All about food, from its history to its production. The chapter on hunger cuts through myths about food aid.

Food Fight: Poets Join the Fight Against Hunger With Poems to Favorite Foods edited and illustrated by Michael J. Rosen (San Diego: Harcourt, Brace and Co., 1996). Young adult. Thirty-three children's poets contribute to the fight against hunger by penning poems about food. Read odes to pies, pizzas, and matzo ball soup.

Organizations

Food Research and Action Center (FRAC)
www.frac.org
202-986-2200
1875 Connecticut Avenue, NW, Suite 540, Washington, DC 20009
Supports research, education, public policy, and programs that work to eradicate hunger. Learn about its "Campaign to End Childhood Hunger."

Hunger 101: A Guide and Activity Workbook
Atlanta Community Food Bank
www.acfb.org/projects/hunger_101/curricula/Hunger_101.pdf
Contains activities to help children learn about poverty and hunger.

Kids Can Make a Difference
www.kidscanmakeadifference.org
An organization to inspire children to help end poverty and hunger. Your children can take a hunger quiz, learn what other kids have to say about hunger, and find out what they can do to help eradicate poverty.

Share Our Strength (SOS)
www.strength.org.
800-969-4767
733 15th Street, NW, Suite 640, Washington, DC 20005
Contact this anti-hunger organization for information and ways to help.

Do Something About Housing and Homelessness

Nearly 40% of all people in the United States without a permanent address tonight will be children. Their average age: nine years old. In fact, families with children make up the fastest-growing segment of the homeless population. Chronic health problems, stunted growth, emotional and behavioral problems, and below-average reading skills are the price these kids likely will pay for their unhappy living situation. Children end up homeless for any number of reasons—parents fleeing abuse, apartments condemned or burned down, chemical dependency or mental health issues, or a family crisis or job layoff that prevents a family from making rent payments. But the single biggest factor is lack of affordable housing.

Dawnette Whitego, 22, and her two sons, Trayvon Whitego, 4, and Samontae James, 2, have lived in a homeless shelter for almost 4 months. Dawnette, a single parent, is working on her GED by attending classes from 9 a.m. to 3 p.m. each day. Every morning she tries to get her children on a bus to a Head Start program specifically designed for homeless children, but for the last two weeks there's been no room for the boys. And when the boys don't go on that bus, Whitego doesn't go to school. "I tell my teacher that I'm staying at the shelter and if they don't get to go to school, I don't have anybody to watch them," says Whitego wearily. Any other daycare arrangement is out of the question because Dawnette's entire $532 monthly welfare grant is taken by the county to pay for her family's stay at the shelter.

Whitego is still hoping to have her GED soon. She'd like to attend a local community college for a nursing assistant's degree, but that seems unlikely. "I'll probably end up getting my GED and just working," says Whitego with resignation. Landlords simply won't rent to someone who only has money from the aid office, even if she could afford the rent and utilities. Yet with only a high school diploma, the kinds of jobs awaiting Whitego will ensure continued poverty for herself and her children.

From advocating for affordable housing to working at a shelter, your family can help.

Ideas for Doing Something About Homelessness

☀ Help at your local shelter. To learn the locations of the shelters in your area, contact First Call for Help, your local United Way, or your state department of human services.

First Call for Help
www.211.org
This United Way-sponsored 24-hour referral service can provide information on the location of food banks, homeless shelters, and other support services. The United Way is working to make 211 the health and human services information number throughout the United States. If that is not currently the number where you live, call your local United Way to find out how to contact First Call for Help in your community.

United Way of America
www.unitedway.org
703-836-7112
701 North Fairfax Street, Alexandria, VA 22314

Call to find out which types of volunteer work are most needed. Here are some possible volunteer opportunities:

● Assist with parties, games, and special events at a shelter for families.

● Help with shelter maintenance. Volunteers can make repairs, paint, and generally fix up a local shelter.

● Establish a library. Collect donated books and ask about a space in the shelter that might be converted into a library.

● Sort and organize donated items. Often, shelters get donations of used clothing, toiletries, and toys, but they need help organizing the donations to distribute to their guests.

● Tutor children. Shelters often run educational programs. If your children are teenagers, all of you can help younger kids at the shelter with homework and other educational activities.

- Transport residents to appointments.

- Assist with office work, including answering phones and processing paperwork.

- Volunteer at the front desk and greet guests as they arrive.

- Teach a life skill, such as resumé writing.

- Help the staff by volunteering to work an overnight shift.

- Help maintain the shelter's web page.

FACTS ABOUT HOMELESSNESS

- Children under age 18 account for 1 out of 4 homeless people.
- Families with children make up about 40% of homeless people.
- A minimum-wage worker would have to work about 87 hours each week to afford a two-bedroom apartment at 30% of his or her income, which is the federal definition of affordable housing.
- Compared with housed poor children, homeless children experience worse health; more developmental delays; more anxiety, depression, and behavioral problems; and lower educational achievement.
  Source: National Coalition for the Homeless Fact Sheets #3 and #7, www.nationalhomeless.org.
- Become affordable housing advocates.
  - Write letters about affordable housing issues to government officials and the media.
  - Attend local meetings to advocate for affordable housing, shelters, and prevention programs.
  - Join the Grassroots Action Network of the National Alliance to End Homelessness (www.naeh.org).
  Source: U.S. Conference of Mayors. A Status Report on Hunger and Homelessness in America's Cities: 1998.

statistics

☼ Donate items to a homeless shelter. Call a local homeless shelter and ask what they need. Popular items include toiletries, diapers, socks, and towels. Then take the family on a shopping trip to buy them. (You might agree to have each member of the family donate part of their earnings or allowance to help pay for the items.) Deliver the items when it is convenient for the shelter workers.

☼ Collect toys for kids in a shelter. Help your children go through their toys and pick out the items they've outgrown. Make sure the toys are in good shape. Call a local shelter or battered women's home and ask if they need toy donations. Consider dropping off the toys when the children will be there so that your children can have a chance to play with them.

- Babysit for children at a battered women's shelter. Often, the women in these shelters must spend their days looking for jobs and housing, or they simply need a break. Your family can provide these children with some safe, nurturing time either at the shelter or at your own home.

- Adopt a room at a shelter. Add touches that will make one of the rooms more homelike, such as a new shower curtain or a coat of paint. Be responsible for the upkeep of the room.

- Organize a drive to collect mittens, scarves, and hats. Donate them to a local homeless shelter, or send them to Hats 4 The Homeless, a charitable organization that provides hats, mittens, and scarves for the homeless in New York City during the holidays.

Hats 4 The Homeless
www.hats4thehomeless.org

- Organize a fundraiser for a local shelter. See Chapter 7 to learn more about planning a fundraising event.

- Create a list of places where the homeless and hungry can get food and shelter. Make copies and give them to needy people you meet on the street.

- Take homeless children on field trips. Trips to the zoo, museum, or library are important educational experiences for youngsters, and children who are homeless often miss out. Fill the void and provide an afternoon of fun for all of you. Contact your local shelter for families to find out how to arrange this.

- Help a homeless family that has just found housing. When a family is moving out of a shelter, some support and practical help can aid them in their transition. You might provide transportation, child care, or referrals to services. Call a local shelter about being matched with a family.

- Help repair and revitalize homes. Thousands of low-income homeowners have difficulty finding resources for the repair and upkeep of their homes. Work to fix leaky roofs, paint, and haul trash to revitalize the homes of low-income homeowners and non-profit facilities. Rebuilding Together, a national organization dedicated to rehabilitating homes and communities, sponsors "National Rebuilding Day" on the last Saturday in April when volunteers and skilled tradespeople join together to repair homes and buildings. Some affiliates work other times during the year as well. If there is no affiliate in your area, ask how you can start one.

Rebuilding Together
www.rebuildingtogether.org
800-4-REHAB-9 or 202-483-9083
1536 16th Street, NW, Washington, DC 20036-1402

☼ Help build houses. Help construct homes with the help of those who will live in them. Habitat for Humanity partners with those in need to build affordable homes. According to its website, "Since 1976, Habitat has built more than 100,000 houses in more than 80 countries, including some 30,000 houses across the United States." The online directory can point you to the Habitat office nearest you.

Habitat for Humanity
www.habitat.org
229-924-6935, ext. 2551 or 2552
121 Habitat Street, Americus, GA 31709

HELPING HANDS

Spending a week scraping, painting, and doing yard work together can be the perfect opportunity to enhance family communication—and that includes lots of laughing, says Oak Grove, Minnesota, mom Barb Anderson. She, her husband, John, and their two sons, David, 14, and Bobby, 16, worked with the Grand Rapids Area Service Project (GRASP) in Michigan fixing up abandoned houses and making home repairs for elderly citizens. Other high school students and adults from the United Methodist Church in St. Francis, Minnesota, joined them for six days of hard work and good times. The volunteers slept in a church basement and took showers at a nearby retirement center. But each night they made time for fun, with go-karting and volleyball being the favorite after-hours activities. "The thing that I like about it is that you have something to work on together," says Anderson. "We're away from the general activities of life. We're only there to work and serve. And we have great conversations while we work. That's the most valuable part."

volunteering

Resources for Doing Something About Homelessness

Books for Kids

Fly Away Home by Eve Bunting, illustrated by Ronald Himler (New York: Clarion Books, 1993). Ages 5-8. This story of a boy and his father living in the airport will make the idea of homelessness real to young children.

The Lady in the Box by Anne McGovern, illustrated by Marni Backer (New York: Turtle Books, 1999). Ages 4-8. Two children help a homeless woman by providing food and warm clothing.

A Rose for Abby by Donna Guthrie, illustrated by Dennis Hockerman (Nashville: Abingdon Press, 1998). Ages 4-8. Abby has an idea that everyone in the community has something to offer the poor.

Sophie and the Sidewalk Man by Stephanie S. Tolan, illustrated by Susan Avishai (New York: Simon and Schuster, 1992). Ages 7-10. Sophie weighs her compassion for a homeless man against her desire for a small stuffed hedgehog. Simple and realistic.

America's Homeless Children: An Educated Reader for Elementary School Kids. Find it online at http://www.nationalhomeless.org/fmn2001/Elementary.pdf.

Homeless by Bernard Wolf (New York: Orchard Books, 1995). Ages 9-12. The story of 8-year-old Mikey's stay in a New York City emergency shelter.

No Place to Be: Voices of Homeless Children by Judith Berck (Boston: Houghton Mifflin Co., 1992). Young adult. Weaves together commentary on homelessness with photos and the words of homeless kids.

Books for Parents

52 Ways to Help Homeless People by Gray Temple (Nashville, TN: Thomas Nelson Publishers, 1991). Young adult and adult. Ideas for helping the homeless, with an emphasis on education and social action.

54 Ways You Can Help the Homeless by Charles A. Kroloff (West Orange, NJ: MacMillan Publishing Co., 1993). Young adult and adult. Lots of suggestions on how to fight homelessness. There's a special section on what children can do.

Organizations and Websites

Catholic Charities USA
www.catholiccharitiesusa.org.
703-549-1390
1731 King Street, Alexandria, VA 22314
This network of social service agencies provides services to needy people and works for social justice.

Kids Next Door
www.hud.gov/kids
By visiting the "Meet Cool People" page at this Housing and Urban Development (HUD) site, kids will get a short, simple, and informative explanation of homelessness and what they can do to make a difference.

National Alliance to End Homelessness
www.naeh.org
202-638-1526
1518 K Street NW, Suite 206, Washington, DC 20005

An organization fighting to eradicate the causes of homelessness. Online, see how you can become a partner (at no fee), join the grassroots action network, or find age-appropriate fact sheets with activities and resources. The group's 10-year plan to end homelessness urges communities to focus on eliminating homelessness rather than simply managing it.

National Coalition for the Homeless
www.nationalhomeless.org
202-737-6444
1012 14th Street, NW, #600, Washington, D.C.20005-3471

A helpful source of information on homelessness. You'll find fact sheets, ways to volunteer, and even a list of children's books on homelessness.

Volunteers of America
www.voa.org

With offices throughout the United States, VOA provides services to the elderly, disabled, homeless, and families and children. The website offers ideas for service and advocacy work and will help you locate the office near you.

Support International Relief Efforts

If your kids have seen the ads on television encouraging viewers to sponsor a child overseas, they're probably aware that many of the world's children live in extreme poverty. Maybe they've mentioned wanting to help out. A sponsorship program is, in fact, one way your family might contribute to international relief efforts.

Poverty exists when people lack the opportunities for development. And while the cycle of poverty is difficult to break, there are successful efforts being made. Examples include programs that increase employment and educational opportunities, address gender inequality, and solve basic health needs. A world in which there is such a dramatic disparity between the haves and have-nots can never be just or stable. Here's how your family can help make a difference around the world.

Ideas for Supporting International Relief Efforts

☀ Sponsor a child overseas. The sponsor family agrees to pay about $24 per month to support community projects where the sponsored child lives, such as building a school or a community clinic. In return, the family receives a picture and description of the child and periodic updates and letters. The sponsor can in turn write letters to the child and sometimes send gifts. Learn about an organization before beginning a sponsorship program.

Save the Children
www.savethechildren.org
800-728-3843
54 Wilton Road, Westport, CT 06880

Christian Children's Fund
www.christianchildrensfund.org
800-776-6767
2821 Emerywood Parkway, Richmond, VA 23294

Childreach
www.childreach.org
800-556-7918
155 Plan Way, Warwick, RI 02886

Children International
www.children.org
800-888-3089
P.O. Box 219055, Kansas City, MO 64121

World Vision
www.worldvision.org
888-511-6598
P.O. Box 9716, Federal Way, WA 98063

☼ Work for the Heifer Project. This organization donates animals to families in poverty in order to make them self-sufficient. Your family can volunteer at one of the three Heifer centers (California, Arkansas, and Massachusetts), raise funds for the organization, or talk about Heifer's mission to community groups. Also, you and your kids can buy an animal to donate to a family in need. (It's a fun way for children to give to charity.) See Heifer's catalog for all the possibilities.

Heifer International
World Headquarters
www.heifer.org
800-422-0474 or 501-907-2600
P.O. Box 8058, Little Rock, AK 72203

☼ Start a new chapter of Free the Children. This kid-initiated organization encourages children and their adult friends to work in support of kids' issues (child labor, child poverty, education). The group defines a "chapter" as two or more people who want to take action. Your family can be a chapter!

Kids Can Free The Children-USA
www.freethechildren.org
800-203-9091
Kids Can Free The Children (International Office)
905-760-9382
Suite 300, 7368 Yonge Street, Thornhill, Ontario, L4J 8H9

☀ Work in one of the chapter offices of UNICEF, which promotes the survival, protection, and development of all children worldwide through fundraising, advocacy, and education. Or, you can organize a "Trick or Treat for UNICEF" campaign in your community.

UNICEF National Office
www.unicefusa.org
800-FOR-KIDS
333 East 38th Street, New York, NY 10016

☀ Volunteer for Church World Service. This is a global relief, development, and refugee agency, the cooperative effort of 36 Protestant, Orthodox, and Anglican denominations in the United States. You can help through this agency in a number of ways.

- Take part in the locally organized Crop Walks throughout the country to raise money for local organizations that fight hunger as well as international relief efforts. Or start a Crop Walk in your community. For more information, call 1-888-CWS-CROP (1-888-297-2767).

- Put together health, baby, or school kits for people in need, called "Gifts of the Heart." See the website for a guide to assembling the kits.

- Take action against poverty and hunger by speaking out through letters, faxes, and e-mails. Check the website to find the current issues that require action.

Church World Service
www.churchworldservice.org
800-297-1516
28606 Phillips Street, P.O. Box 968, Elkhart, IN 46515

☀ Volunteer for an international relief organization. Even if you aren't able to take a trip abroad to help fight poverty, you can still do your part. Here are some ways you might contribute.

- Organize or coordinate a fundraising event (See Chapter 7).

- Help maintain the organization's website.

- Assist with clerical work.

- Give presentations to churches or business and professional organizations.

☀ Donate to the hungry for free. If you have access to the Internet, you can donate money to the hungry every day—and it doesn't cost a thing. Have the family member who turns the computer on in the morning click on www.hungersite.com. Or make it a ritual each evening after dinner or before bed. Every time you visit, sponsors give money for food to the hungry in exchange for their banner being displayed on the site.

☼ Join Feed the Children. For $8 a month, this organization will send you updates on the children whose lives have been affected by your gift. Perhaps each child in your family can earn a few dollars each month to contribute and you can read the updates together at dinner.

Feed the Children
www.feedthechildren.org
800-227-4556
P.O. Box 36, Oklahoma City, OK 73101

☼ Collect and donate shoes and socks to orphanages in the United States and over 25 countries. Shoes for Orphan Souls will tell you what styles and sizes are most needed and where to send them.

Shoes for Orphan Souls
www.shoesfororphansouls.org
877-7ORPHAN (767-7426)

☼ Advocate for debt relief for the poorest countries. It's critical that the poorest countries redirect money used for debt payments toward food, water, education and health care. According to the World Development Movement (WDM), "The lives of seven million children a year could be saved if debt repayments were diverted to health and education." Write your representatives in Congress and ask them to support debt relief for developing countries.

☼ Write letters, e-mails, or faxes in support of international labor rights. The International Labor Rights Fund posts urgent action appeals on its website.

International Labor Rights Fund
www.laborrights.org
202-347-4100
733 15th Street, NW, #920, Washington, DC 20005

☼ Work to ensure a fair wage for all workers. Educate your family about the issue and then write an article or letter to the editor in support of fair trade. For more ways to help, contact Fair Trade Resource Network and Global Exchange.

Fair Trade Resource Network
www.fairtraderesource.org
202-234-6797
P.O. Box 33772, Washington, DC 20033-3772

Global Exchange
www.globalexchange.org
415-255-7296
2017 Mission Street, Suite 303, San Francisco, CA 94110

Resources for Supporting International Relief Efforts

Books for Kids

Beatrice's Goat by Page McBrier, illustrated by Lori Lohstoeter (New York: Simon and Schuster, 2001). Ages 5-8. The story of how a goat from the Heifer Project changes the life of a young girl's family in a small African village.

The Caged Birds of Phnom Penh by Frederick Lipp, illustrated by Ronald Himler (New York: Holiday House, 2001). Ages 4-8. An inspiring story of hope, with beautiful watercolor illustrations.

A Life Like Mine: How Children Live Around the World by Dorling Kindersley Publishing (London: DK Publishing Inc., 2002). Ages 9-12. Readers learn what life is like for children around the world. Lots of photographs.

UNICEF by Katherine Prior (New York: Scholastic Inc., 2001). Ages 9-12. A description of the history, mission, and programs of UNICEF. The photographs and text also educate readers about the challenges children face in developing countries.

Soulmates: A Novel to End World Hunger by John Henry Ballard, illustrated by Roseanne Litzenger (Mill Valley, CA: World Citizens, 1998). Young adult. When a teenager's class sponsors a child in India, it leads to an eye-opening trip to the country. Inspirational.

Taste of Salt: A Story of Modern Haiti by Frances Temple (New York: HarperCollins, 1994). Young adult. Seventeen-year-old Djo tells the story of his life of hardship and poverty with social reformer Father Jean-Bertrand Aristide.

Organizations

Bread for the World
www.bread.org
800-82-BREAD or 202-639-9400
50 F Street, NW, Suite 500, Washington, DC 20001

This Christian organization lobbies for the world's hungry. Visit its website to get the facts on hunger and to learn what you can do to make a difference. Receive a free booklet called "What You Can Do to End Hunger."

Church World Service
Educational Materials
www.churchworldservice.org
Find study guides on global issues, a story called "Hunger Decisions" that provides a look at the difficult choices people in poverty must make, and other poverty education activities for children.

NetAid
www.netaid.org
212-537-0500
267 Fifth Avenue, 11th Floor, New York, NY 10016
This group connects people (primarily through the Internet) who want to help with international relief projects.

Oxfam America
www.oxfamamerica.org
800-77-OXFAM
This organization seeks long-term, worldwide solutions to poverty, hunger, and injustice. It has fact sheets on important poverty-related issues and suggestions on how to make a difference. Learn about hosting a "hunger banquet" in which guests become dramatically aware of the inequities of food distribution. And download a copy of "Just Add Consciousness: A Guide to Social Activism."

Rehydration Project
www.rehydrate.org
P.O. Box 1, Samara, 5235, Costa Rica
Did you know that dehydration kills a child every 14 seconds? This organization is working to change that. Learn the facts and find out what you can do to help.

Building Community 6

There was something unusual about the people who lived in Roseto, Pennsylvania. The citizens of this small Italian-American community had a significantly lower rate of heart attacks than residents of other parts of eastern Pennsylvania or the nation as a whole. This despite a diet high in saturated fat, and smoking and exercise patterns that were nothing out of the ordinary. The reason for Roseto's good health, researchers discovered, was the tight social ties that held the community together. The residents were strongly connected to church, family, and each other. It was this cohesiveness that kept them healthy. Other, larger scale research supports this conclusion. A study of over 6,000 California residents found that socially isolated people had two to three times the mortality rate of those who were socially connected (Berkman and Syme, 1979).

Community really does matter. People who establish bonds with one another are healthier, happier, and live longer. And by volunteering in your community, you and your family can build your own network of connections while strengthening the sense of community for others. Look around your neighborhood and your town. Get to know your community and see what needs to be done. Ask people in your local museums, schools, libraries, and cultural centers how you can contribute. Then get involved, get connected, and make a difference.

Strengthen Your Neighborhood

In Ellen David Friedman's neighborhood of East Montpelier, Vermont, a dozen or so families have gathered for regular communal dinners for the past 15 years. The host household prepares a meal for the families that are available that evening—including infants and great-grandparents, physicians and labor organizers, new arrivals and long-time residents. Together they talk, reflect, laugh, and share. "The children have an extended family here. They have relationships with people of different ages, needs, and requirements. And there's constant mutual aid going on," says Friedman. "It's just about the healthiest antidote there is to the current alienation in society."

Consider your own neighborhood. What would make it a safer and more welcoming place? What might you do to build camaraderie and connect the generations? How can you promote a strong, cohesive community? You and your neighbors are in the best position to improve the quality of life, prevent crime, and support one another by doing such things as keeping children occupied after school, teaching safety tips, cleaning graffiti, or forming a neighborhood group. And these efforts make a difference. Neighborhoods that are both friendly and vigilant are much less likely to experience crime and much more likely to consider their communities to be livable places than places where residents don't know one another.

Ideas for Strengthening Your Neighborhood

☀ Clean up your neighborhood. Pick up litter, remove graffiti (see page 103), and fix up rundown areas. Take pride in your neighborhood's appearance.

☀ Welcome new neighbors. Greet people who are new to your neighborhood and make them feel welcome by baking and delivering a pan of brownies or hosting a neighborhood greeting party. Your family might also put together a packet for new neighbors that includes a map, a list of residents and their phone numbers, and a pamphlet of what to do around town.

☀ Organize a neighborhood block party. This is a great way to meet your neighbors and enjoy a summer evening outside. Apply for a permit to close off the street. Set an appropriate date with a group of other neighbors. Invite your neighbors in person or pass out flyers. Organize games (tug of war, relays, water balloon toss), food (pot-luck or everyone bring their own), and events. Call the fire department and ask if they'll bring a truck for the kids to climb on. Or have a kids' bike parade in which everyone decorates his or her bike and rides it up and down the street.

☀ Start a neighborhood garden and share the bounty. This is a wonderful project that allows neighbors to get to know one another, provides fresh food, keeps children and teens busy with productive work, and beautifies the neighborhood. Get permission from the owner of the garden spot, make a garden plan, and recruit neighbors to help. Contact the American Community Gardening Association for practical information on starting a neighborhood flower or vegetable garden. Also read the *Jumbo Book of Gardening* by Karyn Morris, illustrated by Jane Kurisu (New York: Kids Can Press, 2000).

American Community Gardening Association
www.communitygarden.org
540-552-5550
1916 Sussex Road, Blacksburg, VA 24060

National Gardening Association
www.kidsgardening.com
800-LETSGROW
1100 Dorset Street, South Burlington, VT 05403

☼ Raise money for neighborhood improvements. Maybe your neighborhood needs some playground equipment, a park bench, or new trees. (For ideas on how to raise money, see page 133.)

☼ Work to turn a vacant lot into a park or playing field. If the city owns the property, you will need permission from local authorities to use the lot. If it's a private owner, ask if your family or neighborhood group can use the land. You'll need to raise money for the project and gather volunteers to do the work. (See page 133 for fundraising ideas.)

☼ Help refurbish the neighborhood playground, community center, or park building. This may take more than one family. Ask the appropriate authority if you can paint the building, repair equipment, or build new structures, and then organize a group to accomplish the tasks.

☼ Organize a community festival or help out at one. Organize a "Picnic in the Park" or similar event. Include booths, carnival games, and lots of food. It's a fun way to bring the neighborhood together.

☼ Join or start a neighborhood association or council. This can be an organization focused on getting to know one another, working on projects, or lobbying for neighborhood improvements. The website for the Citizens Committee for New York City offers helpful tip sheets on starting a neighborhood association and other community-building ideas.

Citizens Committee for New York City
www.nyselfhelpguide.org/tips/tip1013403331-1313.html

☼ Join or start a neighborhood watch group. Contact your local police department or the organization listed below for support and information. They may send someone to meet with your group to present techniques for keeping watch. Request signs that designate your neighborhood as having an active watch group. View the online publications, "Starting a Neighborhood Watch" and "Neighborhood Watch Organizers' Guide."

National Crime Prevention Council
www.ncpc.org
202-466-6272
1000 Connecticut Avenue, NW, 13th Floor, Washington, DC 20036

☼ Take part in National Night Out. This crime-prevention program is a one-night-a-year event when neighbors get outside to show their sense of camaraderie and neighborhood spirit. You can organize a block party, cookout, or parade.

National Association of Town Watch
www.nationaltownwatch.org
800-NITE-OUT
P.O. Box 303, Wynnewood, PA 19096

☼ Become a McGruff House. Volunteer to be a "safe" house for children in your neighborhood to go if they're lost or frightened.

National McGruff House Network
www.mcgruffhouse-truck.org or www.ncpc.org
801-486-8768
66 East Cleveland Avenue, Salt Lake City, UT 84115

McGruff Program
www.mcgruff.org

This kid-centered site provides great information on safety, dealing with bullies, and using the Internet safely. It's a fine resource for parents, too, with tips on everything from bicycle safety to helping kids stay home alone safely.

☼ Organize a KidCare ID event. At these events, children are issued booklets with identifying information to be used by law enforcement if they should become missing.

National Center for Missing & Exploited Children
www.missingkids.org
800-662-8337
699 Prince Street, Alexandria, VA 22314
To order a KidCare kit, call 1-800-343-5000.

☼ Organize an event that allows children to turn in toy weapons. Perhaps neighbors or a corporate sponsor could donate toys for children to choose in exchange for their toy weapons. A certificate from the police department or one you've created yourself might also be used as an incentive. For assistance and support and to order "Toys for Peace: A How-To Guide for Organizing Violent Toy Trade-Ins," contact The Lion & Lamb Project.

The Lion & Lamb Project
www.lionlamb.org
301-654-3091
4300 Montgomery Avenue, Suite 104, Bethesda, MD 20814

☼ Organize families in your neighborhood to take part in monthly volunteer projects. Here are some ideas for projects from the Kids Who Care Club in Ladera Ranch, California.

● Pick crops to donate to a homeless shelter.

● Bake cookies and clean walls and playground equipment for a Ronald McDonald House.

- Put on a crazy, zany fashion show and bingo party at a senior center.

- Plant trees in the community.

For more ideas, inspiration, and help getting started, contact Kids Who Care.

Kids Who Care
www.kids-who-care.org

☼ Join or start a neighborhood graffiti removal team. Reducing vandalism and graffiti actually helps prevent bigger crimes from occurring. First, report all graffiti to the police. Meet as often as you need to, and be sure to bring supplies such as heavy gloves, paint solvent, and steel wool. Products are sometimes available free at your local police or fire stations. A Minneapolis website has general information on graffiti removal and prevention.

City of Minneapolis
www.ci.minneapolis.mn.us/graffiti

☼ Petition for what your neighborhood needs. Maybe you have a broken streetlight, or want to install speed bumps or a traffic light. Perhaps a crosswalk needs to be added. Organize your neighbors to get it done. (For more advocacy tips, see page 127.)

☼ Volunteer to distribute and install smoke detectors. Most fire deaths occur in homes with no working smoke detectors. Check with your neighbors to be certain they have working smoke detectors. Offer to install detectors, change batteries, or check to see if they're working. Once you've installed one, check periodically to change the batteries. Your family could also offer to install deadbolt locks, chain locks, and peepholes for elderly residents. Or, you could distribute material on safety to your neighbors at your block party or go door to door. For help in creating a brochure or handout, check with the National Crime Prevention Council.

National Crime Prevention Council
www.ncpc.org
202-466-6272
1000 Connecticut Avenue, NW, 13th Floor, Washington, DC 20036

☼ Help with disaster relief. Contact the American Red Cross to find out how your community can rally together in emergency, such as a hurricane, flood, or tornado. You can raise money, donate needed items, make food for rescue workers, help with cleanup, or volunteer your time in other useful ways.

American Red Cross
www.redcross.org
202-303-4498
2025 E Street, NW, Washington, DC 20006

NEIGHBORLY LOVE

The fire changed everything for the residents of Durango, Colorado. Seventy thousand acres burned in the summer of 2002, including many homes. About two weeks into the fire, Karen Leavitt and her three children (Carson, 9, Sarah, 8, and Margo, 3) walked into Helping Hands, a new organization established to provide aid for families left homeless by the fire, and asked how they could contribute. The family went to work immediately. While Karen problem solved (how to find enough shoelaces for the firefighters), her children sorted donated clothes, comforted kids who'd lost their belongings, and ran errands. Even Margo found a role "testing" the donated toys and cheering up shaken residents who found some comfort in her smile and enthusiasm. For two straight weeks, the family spent each day, all day, doing what needed to be done. "Now we will be like any other Durango family with one critical exception," says Leavitt. "We will always be ready to answer a call for help. Any day. Any time. Any need. Any person."

☼ Make the neighborhood accessible for those with special needs. This might include lobbying for curb cuts in the sidewalk, making appropriate accommodations in community buildings, or patching damaged sidewalks.

Resources for Strengthening Your Neighborhood

Books for Kids

Franklin's Neighborhood by Paulette Bourgeois, illustrated by Brenda Clark (New York: Scholastic, Inc., 1999). Ages 3-8. Franklin learns that the best thing about his neighborhood is the neighbors.

All Around Town: Exploring Your Community Through Craft Fun by Judy Press, illustrated by Karen Weiss (Charlotte, VT: Williamson Publishing Co., 2002). Ages 4-8. Find activities, information, and resources to learn about community sites such as the animal shelter, theater, airport, and senior citizens' center.

City Green by DyAnne DiSalvo-Ryan (New York: Morrow Junior Books, 1994). Ages 4-8. The story of how a community garden brings light and hope into a neighborhood and even changes the outlook of irritable Old Man Hammer.

Grandpa's Corner Store by DyAnne Disalvo-Ryan (New York: HarperCollins, 2000). Ages 4-8. Lucy organizes the community to keep her grandfather's small grocery store from being put out of business by an incoming supermarket. A true celebration of community spirit.

The Green Truck Garden Giveaway: A Neighborhood Story and Almanac by Jacqueline Briggs Martin, illustrated by Alec Gillman (New York: Simon and Schuster, 1997). Ages 5-9. A couple of gardeners in a green truck convert some bored and grumpy neighbors into a community by creating gardens and passing out almanacs. The book includes related tips and anecdotes on everything from the history of pumpkins to plans for a butterfly garden.

Know Your Hometown History: Projects and Activities by Abigail Jungreis (New York: Penguin Group, 1997). Ages 9-12. Here are projects that will give kids the tools to get to know their community's past.

Neighborhood Odes by Gary Soto, illustrated by David Diaz (San Diego: Harcourt Brace Jovanovich, 1992). Ages 9-12. A series of odes to an Hispanic neighborhood in which sprinklers, piñatas, grandparents, and the library are celebrated.

Some Good News by Cynthia Rylant, illustrated by Wendy Halperin (New York: Simon and Schuster, 2001). Ages 9-12. Three nine-year-old cousins start a newspaper about the activities and personalities on Cobble Street, where they live with their Aunt Lucy.

145th Street: Short Stories by Walter Dean Myers (New York: Delacorte Press, 2000). Young adult. Ten stories from a single block in Harlem with rich characters and a powerful sense of community.

Eight Habits of the Heart: Embracing the Values That Build Strong Families and Communities by Clifton L. Taulbert (New York: Penguin Group, 1999). Young adult. Taulbert, who's written well-known memoirs of growing up in the segregated south, presents the wisdom of the people who raised him and explains how their values built a strong community.

Organizations and Websites

Kids and Community
www.planning.org/kidsandcommunity

Kids can learn about city planning and find fun activities that help them learn more about the places where they live.

Law Enforcement Explorers
www.learning-for-life.org/exploring/lawenforcement

This program lets young people between the ages of 14 and 20 volunteer with police departments around the country. Intensive training is involved. This is ideal for students interested in a career in law enforcement. Call your local police department to see if it needs adult help with the program.

Learning Adventures in Citizenship
www.pbs.org/wnet/newyork/laic/fun.html

Would your child like to design a park, solve a community problem, or write poetry in honor of his or her hometown? Kids will find lots of ideas for helping their communities at this PBS website celebrating community.

Reference

Berkman, L, & L. Syme. 1979. "Social Networks, Host Resistance, and Mortality: A Nine-Year Follow-up Study of Alameda County Residents." *American Journal of Epidemiology* 109: 186-204.

Assist Your Neighborhood Schools

We know that when parents participate in school events, develop a working relationship with teachers, and help with homework, kids do better in school. But imagine the benefits if you and your child were to go even further and volunteer together to improve the school—organizing an after-school program, assisting with a fundraiser, or collecting books for the media center. When children are invested in making their school great and see that their families are, too, you send the message that education is important to all of you. This can motivate your child to work harder, both during and after the school day.

Ideas for Assisting Your Neighborhood School

☼ Organize a volunteer club at school. You can organize a club in the local school that meets bi-weekly or monthly to do community service projects. Some activity ideas:

- Have each child collect food from friends and neighbors, and then take it to your local food shelf.

- Each child can earn $5. Then head to the local discount store to buy socks for residents of a homeless shelter.

- Make get-well cards and take the students to distribute them at a hospital.

- Organize a talent show to be performed at a nearby nursing home.

☼ Encourage your school to adopt a charity. Fundraising activities can be focused on the selected charity, as well as service learning opportunities. For instance, if the school chooses to support a school in Haiti, children might learn about the country, its history, and some of the language. (For more information on fundraising, see page 133.)

BEST OF BUDDIES

In 1997, Guilford Primary School in Greensboro, North Carolina had the kind of diversity that would make any school proud. Collectively, the school's 700 students spoke 12 different languages or dialects, including Spanish, French, Russian, and Vietnamese. Kim Taylor, who was president of the school's PTA, was thrilled. But then her neighbor, a Mexican immigrant, told Taylor what a difficult time she had coping with limited English skills when she first arrived in this country. "She said she was afraid to go up to school because she didn't want to look stupid," says Taylor. "I thought, that's awful. We can't have any of our parents coming to school feeling that way." So with the help of the ESOL (English for Speakers of Other Languages) teacher, Taylor initiated BUDDIES, a volunteer program that matched the school's bilingual families with families who spoke little English. The adults helped the non-English-speaking parents translate teacher's notes, assisted them at school and PTA events, and answered questions, while the children of the volunteer families helped their classmates learn their way around the school. "It's a simple program that requires no money," says Taylor. "It's just work from the heart. People reaching out to help others."

volunteering

☼ Read to children. Read with and to school-age students. You and your older children can do this in the mornings if the local elementary school has an earlier start time, or during lunch break. If you're interested in initiating a "Reading Buddies" program in your local school, visit the University of Nevada-Reno's E.L. Cord Foundation Center for Learning and Literacy for helpful advice on getting started.

E.L. Cord Foundation Center for Learning and Literacy
www.unr.edu/cll/reading%20buddies.htm

ORGANIZING SCHOOL FUNDRAISERS

Schools need money, and a fundraiser is everyone's instant answer to getting some. But most of us are tired of buying raffle tickets, selling pizzas, volunteering at bake sales, and purchasing overpriced gift-wrap. However, with a little thought and effort, schools can find fun and enriching ways to earn money. Use these guidelines when evaluating your school's fundraising efforts.

Know where the money will go. Fundraising should only be used to accomplish specific educational goals. Decide what your school needs—maybe to buy tickets to a concert or to start a science fair— then organize a fundraiser to help achieve those objectives.

Don't allow children to solicit money. Many parents object to fundraising efforts that involve children selling items door to door and receiving glitzy prizes for their efforts. They cite a variety of concerns— safety, a distaste for buying (sometimes mediocre) products at inflated prices, and the discomfort of imposing on friends or neighbors to make a purchase. In addition, it's harmful for kids to be continually motivated to raise funds for external rewards rather than because they're contributing to a worthy cause. If your school chooses to sell products, make certain it is clear that the parents, not the children, are responsible for selling.

Choose a fundraiser that is family oriented. Fundraisers such as pizza or spaghetti suppers, pancake breakfasts, ice cream socials, movie nights, or carnivals do more than make money. They foster parent involvement, build ties to the community, and bring families together. Other great fundraising options include read-a-thons, walk-a-thons, or book fairs.

Consider having parents donate money outright. Some schools simply ask for donations and skip the hoopla altogether. Many parents are thrilled with this option.

Put the burden for basic needs on the school district. Parents should advocate at the district or state level for basic items such as playground equipment, computers, library books, or a paraprofessional in the classroom.

Ask foundations or businesses to help out. Make use of community resources to defray expenses and avoid fundraisers. Create successful business partnerships.

volunteering

☀ Organize your child's school to donate books and other school supplies to a school with fewer resources.

☀ Organize a reading competition or reading project in the school. Here are some possibilities:

- Establish a Family Reading Night with activities and games centered on reading.

- If the children in the school collectively log 2,000 hours of reading, the principal agrees to do something silly (for example, dress in a clown outfit or wear pajamas to school).

- Each classroom logs the number of hours that kids read outside of school, and the class with the most hours receives a class pizza party.

- Establish a read-aloud program. Organize parents and community members to take turns reading stories to different classes. Your older children can help with the organization and the reading.

☀ Support your school's media center. You could follow the example at some schools and create a "Friends of the Library" group at your school. Some projects your group might consider: Develop reading lists for each grade, collect books, raise money for new books and technology (including help securing library grants), arrange reading activities and contests, or bring in speakers and performers.

☀ Help the PTA. Maybe your family could work at a carnival, bake and sell goodies for a bake sale, or collect books for a book drive. Everyone in the family can do their part to help raise money for the school. Become part of established fundraisers or initiate your own.

☀ Collect for education. Redeem labels and box tops for educational merchandise. Ask if your school participates in any of these fundraisers. If not, maybe you could get the program started:

Campbell's Labels for Education	www.labelsforeducation.com
General Mills Boxtops for Education	www.boxtops4education.com
Target School Fundraising Program	www.target.com/target_group/ schools/search_school.jhtml

Holders of Target Guest Cards can designate 1% of purchases to their favorite school.

☼ Start a support group. Establish a support group for kids struggling with an issue your family can help with, such as divorce, bullying, or Attention Deficit Disorder. Talk to the school's guidance counselor, psychologist, or social worker for help and information.

☼ Start a peer mediation program. Peer mediators are student volunteers who have been taught to serve as peacemakers in their schools. They work in the classroom or on the playground to solve disputes between students. This program, used by a growing number of schools, has helped create a more respectful atmosphere and has decreased the number of fights in schools. The Colorado School Mediation Project provides helpful information.

The Colorado School Mediation Project
www.csmp.org/programs/peermed/peer_home.htm

☼ Tutor children. If you have older children, volunteer together to assist children in elementary school with their homework either after or before school. If there's not such a program in your area, consider starting one.

☼ Volunteer at Head Start. Volunteers are critical to Head Start, an early-childhood program for at-risk preschoolers. Your family might assist with classroom activities or parent education or donate goods and services. To find the Head Start program nearest you, check the phone book or visit the Head Start Bureau website.

Head Start
www.acf.hhs.gov/programs/hsb

☼ Donate an instrument to the school's music program. Are you hiding instruments that haven't been played in years under your bed or in your closets? Donate them to a school so that all children can have the opportunity to make music.

☼ Assist coaches for school sports. Do you and your daughter love soccer? Maybe the two of you could help out with a soccer team.

☼ Honor teachers. Recognize the special contributions of particular teachers with a school assembly, gift, ceremony, or party. You might want to schedule the event for national Teacher Appreciation Week, which is sponsored by the National Parent Teacher Association (PTA).

Parent Teacher Association
www.pta.org

☼ Find speakers for your local school. Individuals in your community have much to share with children. Why not help the school bring these folks to speak to the students? Speak with the school's parent-teacher association and the faculty to see what types of talents they would like to share with the children. Then your family can begin making phone calls and arrangements.

☼ Offer to teach an after-school class. What talents does your family possess? Do you love to knit, take pictures, speak Spanish, or juggle? Why not teach some children to share your passion? Contact your local school district about teaching a class. If your school doesn't offer after-school classes, maybe you could start a program.

☼ Photograph kids for a school newsletter. This is a fun activity and a way for your whole family to get to know the kids in your child's school. Check with school administrators to determine if they have parental permission for publishing photographs of students.

Resources for Assisting Your Neighborhood School

Organizations and Websites

Communities In Schools
www.cisnet.org
703-519-8999 or 800-CIS-4KIDS
277 South Washington Street, Suite 210, Alexandria, VA 22314
Helps connect schools with community resources to provide students with what they need to succeed, including marketable skills, a relationship with a caring adult, and community service opportunities.

National PTA
www.pta.org
800-307-4PTA (4782) or 312-670-6782
330 N. Wabash Avenue, Suite 2100, Chicago, IL 60611
Locate your state PTA office, find tips for helping your child succeed, check out the child and family web guide, and learn how to get involved in your child's school.

Support Libraries and Literacy

We all know someone who spent his or her early years in the library or someone for whom books were his or her salvation, an escape from a difficult childhood. Isaac Asimov, the well-known and prolific science fiction writer was one of those children. He writes in *I, Asimov* (1994),

> *"I received the fundamentals of my education in school, but that was not enough. My real education, the superstructure, the details, the true architecture, I got out of the public library. For an impoverished child whose family could not afford to buy books, the library was the open door to wonder and achievement, and I can*

never be sufficiently grateful that I had the wit to charge through that door and make the most of it. Now, when I read constantly about the way in which library funds are being cut and cut, I can only think that the door is closing and that American society has found one more way to destroy itself."

Libraries can play a critical role in a child's life—and in the lives of adults, too. Libraries provide information and entertainment at a price everyone can afford. They're absolutely free. And, according to a 2002 American Library Association survey, 91% of us still believe the library has a vital role to play in the community, even with the advent of the Internet (www.ala.org). If your family loves libraries and books, you can help keep them strong.

Ideas for Supporting Libraries and Literacy

☼ Have a used book sale. Collect books from neighbors and friends. Have a sale and donate the proceeds to the library or a local literacy group. Or simply donate the books and videotapes to the library.

☼ Donate books to those in need. Set up a bin inside a bookstore and encourage people to contribute children's books. Ask the owner or manager of a local bookstore if your family can set up and maintain a bin for patrons to contribute new children's books they've purchased. Empty the bin periodically and donate the books to a shelter, library, children's hospital, or to one of the organizations listed below. Some organizations will take high-quality used books. Others ask you to purchase new books to send.

Books for Africa	**www.booksforafrica.org** **651-602-9844**
Boaters for Books, Inc.	**www.boatersforbooks.org**
Page Ahead	**www.pageahead.org** **206-461-0123**
Books Through Bars	**www.booksthroughbars.org** **215-727-0882**
The Prison Book Project	**www.btp.tao.ca**

☼ Start a story hour at your local library. If your library doesn't offer a story time for preschoolers, your family could organize one.

☼ Call your local library to find out how your family can help keep the library running smoothly behind the scenes. Here are some possibilities:

● "Adopt" a shelf, or section of a shelf, to keep in order.

● Rewind videotapes.

- Make decorations and create exhibits.

- Help with special events.

- Wipe off book covers.

- Dust computers.

- Sort and shelve books.

- Repair books.

- Design a display case. Plan the theme, gather the supplies, and write a description of what's included.

☼ Help out at a library's computer center. If your family has computer skills, share them with others by volunteering at the computer center at your local library. Teach others how to find information using computers.

☼ Help with a library's summer reading program. Libraries play a vital role in helping children retain their academic skills during the school-free months. Many have programs in which kids can receive special charts to record each book read (or read to them) during the summer. Sometimes they offer prizes. Volunteers help sign kids up for the program and hand out prizes.

☼ Volunteer for Reading Is Fundamental. This successful organization provides books to needy children. Your family can help by ordering books for distribution, planning reading events and activities, reading to children, or raising funds.

Reading Is Fundamental
www.rif.org
877-RIF-READ
1825 Connecticut Avenue, NW, Suite 400, Washington, DC 20009

☼ Give a lecture at your library on a subject of interest to your family. Libraries are often a forum for lectures, meetings, and events. Maybe your family has an interest you could share with the community, such as tracing genealogy, making beaded jewelry, or science fiction and fantasy books for teens.

☼ Begin a special collection at the library. Despite an increasing number of immigrants in your community, maybe your library has no books in their native languages. Your family could begin a collection to donate. Or perhaps you'd like to help organize a collection of comic books for kids.

☼ Help in your library's outreach programs. Public libraries often have programs to reach out to the community, such as home delivery services, visits to schools and organizations, interpreters for library programs, mini-branches in senior citizen centers, and book discussion kits. Volunteer to help with an existing program or suggest a new outreach program your library may want to organize.

☼ Become a library advocate. To learn the issues and how to take action to support libraries, visit http://capwiz.com/ala/ and read the "Library Advocates Handbook" online at ala.org. Or you might consider volunteering with Friends of the Library (FOL). These organizations generally raise funds for special library programs and purchases. Contact your local library for information or check out FOL on the Internet.

Friends of the Library
www.folusa.org
800-9-FOLUSA
1420 Walnut Street, Suite 450, Philadelphia, PA 19102

"The library connects us with the insights and knowledge, painfully extracted from Nature, of the greatest minds that ever were, with the best teachers, drawn from the entire planet and from all our history, to instruct us without tiring, and to inspire us to make our own contribution to the collective knowledge of the human species. Public libraries depend on voluntary contributions. I think the health of our civilization, the depth of our awareness about the underpinnings of our culture and our concern for the future can all be tested by how well we support our libraries." *Cosmos* by Carl Sagan (New York: Random House, 1980).

☼ Create a story hour in your neighborhood and read to kids. Volunteer to read books to the children in your neighborhood once each week. While one family member reads, another can act out or use puppets to dramatize the story. You'll give parents a badly needed break and give children the gift of reading.

☼ Help at a literacy program. Many literacy programs use only adults as literacy tutors, but other family members might volunteer as child caretakers so parents can get the tutoring they need. Contact your local literacy program to ask about the possibilities.

America's Literacy Directory
www.literacydirectory.org
800-228-8813

☼ Talk to kids about books. One way to get children interested in books is to give "book talks." This means going into a classroom and sharing your thoughts on books you've discovered. Family members can briefly summarize the book; read an interesting or exciting part; show illustrations from the book; dress, act, or talk like one of the book's characters; and answer questions about the book. This will encourage kids to seek out the book and read.

Resources for Supporting Libraries and Literacy

Books for Kids

Library by Sarah Stewart, illustrated by David Small (New York: Farrar, Straus and Giroux, 1999). Ages 4-8. Passionate reader Elizabeth Brown comes up with a splendid idea for what to do with her too many books.

Tomás and the Library Lady by Pat Mora, illustrated by Raul Colon (New York: Alfred Knopf, 1997). Ages 4-8. This is the inspirational story of Tomás Rivera, former chancellor of the University of California at Riverside, and how a librarian helped him learn the joy of reading as a young boy.

The Inside-Outside Book of Libraries by Julie Cummins, paintings by Roxie Munro (New York: Penguin Books, 1996). Ages 6-10. This book will expand a child's perceptions of libraries. Readers discover that libraries can be found aboard aircraft carriers, in homes, in a single room, and on the busy streets of New York.

Richard Wright and the Library Card by William Miller, illustrated by Gregory Christie (New York: Lee & Low Books, 1999). Ages 6-10. This is a powerful story from the life of author Richard Wright. Readers discover how Wright got access to the magic of books and libraries at a time when they were strictly off limits to African Americans.

Libraries by Lucia Raatma (New York: Grolier Publishing, 1998). Ages 9-12. An informative book describing the types of libraries and their history.

The Library Card by Jerry Spinelli (New York: Scholastic, Inc., 1998). Ages 9-12. Four stories of how a magical library card transforms the lives of kids in need. Fun read from this award-winning children's author.

Books for Parents

Help America Read: A Handbook for Volunteers by Gay Su Pinnell and Irene C. Fountas (Portsmourth, N.H.: Heinemann, 1997). Ten ways literacy volunteers can help children learn to enjoy reading and build literacy skills. If you and your teenage children are teaching kids to read, this book has practical tips to make you more effective.

Organizations and Websites

American Library Association (ALA)
www.ala.org
800-545-2433
50 E. Huron, Chicago, IL 60611
Learn all about libraries and what you can do to support them.

National Institute for Literacy
www.nifl.gov
800-228-8813 (hotline)
202-233-2025

This organization is focused on adult literacy and is therefore less likely to offer family volunteering opportunities. But it is an excellent source of information on literacy. Visit the website or call the national literacy hotline to find literacy programs in your area.

Enhance Arts and Culture

Volunteering for the arts is both popular and fun. According to the American Association of Museums, "For every paid staff member, 2.5 people volunteer their time and services to museums. Of Americans age 18 and older, 1 in 480 is a museum volunteer." (www.aam-us.org/programs/gov_affairs/issues.cfm) Impressive? Yes. However, helping out at a museum is only one way to support the arts. You might also consider volunteering at a history center, or lending a hand at a local theater or art fair. There are dozens of opportunities for your family to help strengthen your community's arts and cultural activities.

Ideas for Enhancing Arts and Culture

- Help out at a gallery or museum. Work at the welcome desk, become a docent, or work in the museum shop. Each family member might take on a different responsibility or work together on one project.

- Volunteer at an arts and crafts fair. Create and distribute posters and flyers or help with set-up, publicity, office work, cleanup, and ticket sales. This can be a great one-time volunteer opportunity. If you're lucky, you'll get some free food and a t-shirt!

- Help out at a local theater. If your children are younger, seek out opportunities at a local children's theater. These organizations may need intermission hosts, ticket sellers, coat-checkers, ticket takers, ushers, publicists, or fundraisers. If you have a specific talent, you might work on costume and set construction or hair and make-up. Sometimes local theaters are even looking for test audiences, which would mean you could attend a free performance.

- Take at-risk kids to a museum, play, or concert. Some children never have the opportunity to attend a theater or music production. Your family can offer to take kids from a homeless shelter or Head Start program to a show.

- Write reviews for a neighborhood newspaper on local cultural events. After your family has attended a performance at a children's theater or a special concert, offer to write a "family review" for a local paper. You can critique the show from different age perspectives.

☀ Work at a science center. You might work as guides or at the information desk, help with special events, assist in the office or computer lab, or help with exhibit design. A usual perk is free passes to the museum. To find the one nearest you, visit the website of the Association of Science-Technology Centers.

Association of Science-Technology Centers
www.astc.org

☀ Support public radio and television. Answer phones during membership drives or work in the office. Some radio stations are completely volunteer owned and operated. You can find your local National Public Radio station by visiting the website listed below. For the Public Broadcasting station near you, check out the PBS website below. Visit the National Federation of Community Broadcasters website for other public radio stations in your area.

National Federation of Community Broadcasters
www.nfcb.org
510-451-8200
1970 Broadway, Suite 1000, Oakland, CA 94612

National Public Radio
www.npr.org
202-513-2000
635 Massachusetts Avenue, NW, Washington, DC 20001

Public Broadcasting
www.pbs.org/stationfinder
703-739-5000
1320 Braddock Place, Alexandria, VA 22314

☀ Perform at a school, nursing home, or senior center. Does your family have a talent to share? Perhaps you sing together, or each of you plays a musical instrument. Share your talent by performing for others. Or, start a community band or chorus. Meet regularly for rehearsal and then volunteer to perform at community events, senior centers, hospitals, or shelters.

☀ Volunteer with your local arts council. Nurture and support local artists. You might help plan activities, fundraise, or work on creating an art directory.

☀ Work at a children's museum. Your family can give presentations, read stories, be roaming greeters, act as arts and crafts facilitators at the drop-in art studio, help maintain the toy library, or work with children on the floor. There might also be opportunities to work in the gift shop or front desk, or clean, repair, and install exhibits. Many museums need help with marketing and preparing bulk mailings. Some museums have parent-child teams volunteering as role models in the museum.

☼ Paint a mural. For the artistically inclined, there are sometimes opportunities to help paint murals on exterior building walls or inside community centers, homeless shelters, bus shelters, or schools. Experienced artists are often needed, but sometimes others are invited to participate. Or add to the One World Mural online. Kids of any age can add words or drawings to an online mural at www.tolerance.org.

☼ Work at a history museum or historic house or site. Love history? Your family can give tours, do research, organize old records, plan exhibits, or take oral histories.

THE ENTERTAINERS

Barry Davis wanted his children to have the same connection to elderly people he'd had growing up in a huge extended family in San Antonio, Texas. His wife, Gail Rosenblum, wanted a chance to give back to the community while spending time with her family. So four years ago, the family started spending one Saturday afternoon each month entertaining seniors during the Shabbat celebration at the Sholom Home in St. Louis Park, Minn. Sydney Davis, now 13, and Noah Davis, 11, take turns playing the piano while their sister, Carly, 4, sings the alphabet, dances, or simply wanders around the room holding hands with the elderly people. Gail and Barry occasionally contribute a song or two, as well. Then everyone helps serve refreshments and visits with the residents. "They're just so thrilled to see children," says Rosenblum. "And the kids have this perfectly attentive audience for their music. Everything they do is delightful to the crowd."

volunteering

☼ Offer to do face painting and body art for children. Contact the local library for a time and space to offer your family's creative talents. Or volunteer your services at a homeless shelter, crisis nursery, or daycare center.

☼ Assist archaeologists in excavating activities in your local area. Try your local historical society, or the anthropology department of a local university or college.

National Park Service Volunteers-In-Parks Program
www.nps.gov/volunteer

Resources for Enhancing Arts and Culture

Books for Kids

Ella's Trip to the Museum by Elaine Clayton (New York: Crown Publishers, Inc., 1996). Ages 4-8. Ella uses her vivid imagination—dancing with the ballerinas in the paintings, frolicking with a statue of a Roman goddess—to make her visit to the museum memorable.

Mrs. Brown on Exhibit and Other Museum Poems by Susan Katz, illustrated by R.W. Alley (New York: Simon and Schuster, 2002). Ages 4-8. A collection of poems from a teacher and her class who love museums. From an insectarium to clocks to a giant heart, kids learn about exhibits in museums all over the country.

Visiting the Art Museum by Laurene Krasny Brown and Marc Brown (New York: E.P. Dutton, 1992). Ages 4-8. A charming look at a family's visit to the museum. See it all—Rousseau, Pollock, mummies, and arms and armor—along with the kind of comments you'd truly hear from kids touring a museum. ("I've seen enough. Let's eat lunch.")

Museums by Patrice Koelsch (Mankato, MN: Creative Company, 2001). Ages 9-12. Learn about the history of museums, what they all have in common, and examples of different types of museums.

Organizations and Websites

American Association of Museums
www.aam-us.org
202-289-1818
1575 Eye Street, NW, Suite 400, Washington, DC 20005
Contains information about museums around the country.

City Search
www.citysearch.com
Want to know about local museums so you can inquire about volunteer opportunities? Curious about whether there's an arts and crafts show coming? Want to get some ideas about where to take a group of homeless kids on an outing? This website can connect you to what's going on in cities all over the country.

Save America's treasures
www.saveamericastreasures.org
202-588-6202 or 877-TREASURES (873-2787)
A partnership of the National Park Service and the National Trust for Historic Preservation, this organization's website describes several ways to help save historic sites.

References

Asimov, I. 1994. *I, Asimov.* New York: Doubleday.

Sagan, C. 1980. *Cosmos.* New York: Random House.

Social Action 7

Once upon a time, some villagers gathered on the banks of a river for a picnic. As they were talking and eating, someone noticed a baby floating down the river. The child was screaming in terror and was clearly going to drown. Several of the townspeople swam out into the water to save the baby. But just as they pulled it to safety, they noticed another baby struggling in the current, and then another. Soon, all the people were mobilized in order to save the babies coming down the river. But suddenly, one villager started dashing upstream along the banks of the river. The other rescuers were incensed. "Where are you going?" they cried. "Stay here and help us save these babies!" "No," came the reply. "Someone needs to stop them from being thrown in." This old story, in its many versions, illustrates the importance of working toward social change. Although every kind of gesture and hour spent helping others makes a difference in the lives of those individuals we serve, concerted and collective action is critical if we want to make fundamental changes in our social and environmental fabric.

As with any type of volunteering, the amount of time you invest in social action is your choice. You could spend 15 minutes a month drafting a letter to your congressperson about global warming or spend hours each week working to get your favorite candidate elected to the state legislature. In both cases, you'll have the satisfaction that comes from being engaged in civic life. Here are ways your family can influence what laws get passed, who gets elected, and how the public responds to issues.

Support Candidates and the Political Process

"Americans' direct engagement in politics and government has fallen steadily and sharply over the last generation, despite the fact that average levels of education—the best individual-level predictor of political participation—have risen sharply throughout this period. Every year over the last decade or two, millions more have withdrawn from the affairs of their communities" (Putnam, 1995).

How can we reverse this trend of disengagement and get citizens involved in the democratic process again? One sure way is to get kids excited about politics. Young people are the voters of tomorrow, so it is critical that they become both educated and involved. If you get your family together to work for the candidates and causes you believe in, you'll not only ensure that we get the office-holders and laws we most need, but you'll be teaching your children to be active, participating citizens.

First, your family must become informed citizens. Winston Churchill once said, "The best argument against democracy is a five-minute conversation with the average voter." In fact, we could all stand to learn more about issues, candidates, and the political process. Here are some ways to become more informed.

- Learn about critical issues. The public library and Internet are good places to start. Also, ask your government representatives for information. Or contact advocacy groups working in particular areas. Your family might want to become "experts" on such areas as gun control, death penalty, foreign affairs, welfare reform, abortion, human rights, education, crime, health, budget and the economy, or immigration. Once you're knowledgeable about an issue, you'll know what needs to be done to make a positive difference.

- Find out who your elected officials are. Visit the League of Women Voters website (www.lwv.org), click on "Get Involved," and enter your zip code to learn the names of your federal, state, and local office holders. Ask for ways your family can volunteer to get out the vote.

  League of Women Voters
  www.lwv.org
  202-429-1965
  1730 M Street, NW, Suite 1000, Washington, DC 20036-4508
  A national organization working to promote democracy through campaign finance reform, education, and civic participation.

- Find out about current federal and state races and learn about pending legislation.

  Democracy Net
  www.dnet.org

- Keep up with current events. Read the newspaper together or make it a habit to watch and discuss the news each evening. But remember that the news can be disturbing to children. Let your child's age and maturity level guide you in determining the kind of news he or she watches. Whenever possible, watch the news together with your son or daughter, and always talk to your child or teen about what you've seen in the newspaper or on television.

☼ Visit your state capitol. Take a family field trip, tour the building, and learn how state laws are made.

☼ Visit Washington, D.C. The biggest challenge is deciding which of the hundreds of sights to visit. Luckily, many of the city's standout attractions sit along a wide grassy expanse known as The Mall, anchored by the Lincoln Memorial at one end and the Capitol at the other. You can also visit the White House, the Holocaust Museum, and the Bureau of Printing and Engraving, along with dozens of other fun and educational sights in Washington.

☼ Learn about American history. Your family can read books about famous Americans and discover how our government was formed.

"The death of democracy is not likely to be an assassination from ambush. It will be a slow extinction from apathy, indifference, and undernourishment."
—*Robert Maynard Hutchins (1899 -1977)*

Ideas for Supporting Candidates and the Political Process

☼ Get out the vote. Voting is critical to democracy. Don't allow others to get apathetic about this fundamental right. Take your children with you to vote so they see the process in action. Also, help people register to vote and transport those who need assistance to the polling places.

www.takeyourkidstovote.org

● Call the League of Women Voters (see information on previous page) and ask for ways your family can volunteer to get out the vote.

● Educate people about the importance of voting by passing out flyers your family has created, writing letters to your local paper urging others to vote, and asking local media to remind voters to exercise their constitutional privilege. Include information about absentee ballots.

● Volunteer to help get people to the polls by offering to drive those who need assistance.

● Join the "You Don't Need a Home to Vote" campaign, which encourages and facilitates voting by the homeless. Go to www.nationalhomeless.org and click on "What You Can Do" for more information.

● Go door to door to register voters.

● Help seniors and others who are unable to get to a polling place on Election Day to obtain absentee ballots.

Initiate, eliminate, or change a law. Perhaps you'd like to see tougher gun control, stiffer penalties for drunk drivers, or stricter environmental regulations. Your family can make a difference by helping create new laws or getting rid of outdated statutes. How you go about it will depend on whether it's a local, state, or federal law. The first step is to learn about lawmaking and how citizens can provide input. You may want to gather information from elected officials and others, collect signatures for a petition, lobby lawmakers (by telephone or in person), and build support for your proposal. To get started, the best easy-to-use guide is *The Kid's Guide to Social Action* by Barbara A. Lewis (Minneapolis: Free Spirit Publishing, 1998). This book explains the difference between local, state, and federal laws and describes the skills you'll need to enact changes.

Work for a candidate your family supports. Call the candidate's office and ask how your family can help. Here are some possibilities:

- Stuff envelopes and do other office work.

- Make telephone calls or answer phones in the campaign office.

- Write an article or letter to the editor for a school or community newspaper in support of your candidate.

- Host a fundraising party.

- Go door to door talking about your candidate.

HISTORY OF VOTING RIGHTS

Many Americans have had to fight hard for the right to vote. Here's a short history of the suffrage movement.

1870: The 15th Amendment granted African-American men the right to vote.

1920: The 19th Amendment was ratified, giving women the right to vote.

1924: Native Americans were given U.S. citizenship, but some states barred them from voting until 1948.

1965: The Voting Rights Act guaranteed equal access to the ballot, especially in the South where African-Americans were often required to pass literacy tests and pay poll taxes in order to vote.

1971: The 26th Amendment lowered the voting age to 18 years. (The voting age had been 21.)

Who Can Vote in the United States?

You must be 18 years old.

You must be a U.S. citizen.

You must be registered to vote.

voting rights

- Go door to door handing out literature.

- Help at special events for the candidate.

- Put up lawn signs and distribute campaign buttons.

- Attend a campaign rally.

Resources for Supporting Candidates and the Political Process

Books for Kids

America: A Patriotic Primer by Lynne Cheney, illustrated by Robin Preiss Glasser (New York: Simon and Schuster, 2002). Ages 4-8. An ABC's of American history and government that celebrates democratic principles and famous figures from our country's past. Contains lots of detailed illustrations.

If I Were President by Catherine Steir, illustrated by DyAnne DiSalvo-Ryan (Morton Grove, IL: Albert Whitman and Co., 1999). Ages 4-8. A kid-friendly introduction to the duties of the President of the United States.

How the U.S. Government Works by Syl Sobel (New York: Barron's Educational Series, Inc., 1999). Ages 9-12. A simple guide to the workings of the U.S. government.

So You Want to Be President? by Judith St. George, illustrated by David Small (New York: Penguin Putnam Books, 2000). Ages 9-12. An entertaining look at our presidents' lives with cartoon illustrations.

You Want Women to Vote, Lizzie Stanton? by Jean Fritz, illustrated by DyAnne DiSalvo-Ryan (New York: Putnam Publishing Group, 1999). Ages 9-12. This biography of 19th-century feminist Elizabeth Cady Stanton is a fun way to learn about the women's suffrage movement and what it takes to stand up for what you believe in.

Don't Know Much About History: Everything You Need to Know About American History but Never Learned by Kenneth C. Davis (New York: Perennial, 2003). Young adult and adult. A fun, readable primer on American history written in a question and answer format.

Politics for Dummies by Ann DeLaney (New York: Wiley Publishing, 2001). Young adult and adult. Basic information for learning about and getting involved in politics.

Teen Power Politics: Make Yourself Heard by Sara Jane Boyers (Brookfield, CT: Twenty-First Century Books, 2000). Young adult. Learn about politics, including voting rights, activism, and the election process, and get inspired to make your voice heard.

Organizations and Websites

Ben's Guide to U.S. Government for Kids
http://bensguide.gpo.gov

Kids can get an overview of the federal government and how it works appropriate to their age level.

PBS Kids Democracy Project
www.pbs.org/democracy/kids

Kids can learn about the role of government, voting, and voting rights.

Kids Newsroom
www.kidsnewsroom.com

Find current events, sports, and entertainment news presented at a kid's eye view.

Kids Voting USA
www.kidsvotingusa.org
480-921-3727 or 800-500-VOTE
398 South Mill Avenue, Suite 304, Tempe, AZ 85281

Voting rates in the United States are abysmally low. This organization is working to involve kids in voting and elections at an early age. Take a look at their "Family Guide" for ideas on how to engage your children in the democratic process.

Project Vote Smart
www.vote-smart.org

Great site for information on candidates' views on the issues. Research internships are available.

Rock the Vote
www.rockthevote.org

Register to vote, find links to dozens of activist websites, and learn about electoral reform at this site for young people.

Time for Kids
www.timeforkids.com

Kids can become informed about current events, play games, and learn about the world.

References

Putnam, R.D. 1995. "Bowling Alone: America's Declining Social Capital." *Journal of Democracy* 6(1): 65-78.

Fight for a Cause

In *250 Ways to Make America Better: Great Ideas on How We Can Improve Our Country* (New York: Villard Books, 1999), the editors of *George* magazine asked Americans what they would do to make our country a better place to live. The contributors discuss everything from animal rights to parent education. A few responses are silly and irreverent, but most are thoughtful and provocative. Have family members take turns reading the responses to each other. Critique the ideas and suggest your own.

That is one way to begin to sort out which issues you and your family feel most passionate about. You might also notice what topics seem to resonate around the dinner table when current events are discussed or which specific community problems or global issue everyone seems most eager to solve. Then learn all you can about it. Get information from the library, Internet, books, and magazine articles. Perhaps each member of the family can research some aspect and report back. If something could use improvement, create a volunteer opportunity for yourselves. On the next page are some of the ways you can fight for your cause.

WHEN A CAUSE FINDS YOU

Sometimes causes find you. Consider the Mullis family, who learned five years ago that their husband/father, Ron, had early-onset Alzheimer's disease. Now, with Ron in a nursing home, Lory and her sons, Zack, 11, and Chris, 9, are doing what they can to provide support to other families who are struggling with the disease. When the Alzheimer's Association asked them to give an interview to a local news station, walk to raise money for research, and participate in a video for fundraising efforts, they were happy to do it. Describing life with their dad now has been therapeutic for the boys, and knowing that they're helping others is gratifying for them, says Lory. "They know we're providing some comfort to other families when they tell their story."

volunteering

GETTING IN TOUCH WITH YOUR LEADERS

To write a letter to your Representative:
Hon._____
U.S. Congress
Washington, D.C. 20515

To write to your Senators:
Senator_____
U.S. Senate
Washington, D.C. 20510

To call your Senators or Representative:
Dial the Capitol switchboard at 202-224-3121 or visit www.senate.gov or
www.house.gov to find their direct numbers.

To write the President:
President _____
The White House
1600 Pennsylvania Avenue NW
Washington, D.C. 20500

To call the White House:
Switchboard: 202-456-1414
Comments: 202-456-1111

To e-mail the President:
president@whitehouse.gov

To write to your Governor, state legislators, or other state officials, look under
"State Government" in your telephone directory.

contacts

Ideas for Fighting for a Cause

☼ Join an organization that works in support of your issue and ask how your family
can help. From the environment to human rights, there are thousands of
organizations working to make a difference on a variety of issues. Find the one
focusing on the issue your family cares most about, and give them a call and ask
how each of you can contribute.

☼ Call or write elected officials. Let your elected officials know what you care about.
According to one activist manual, it only takes 10 to 20 handwritten letters to draw

the attention of a congressperson to a particular issue. Your letters do make a difference. When calling, it is not always necessary to speak directly with the elected official. Simply let the staffer know your opinion on an issue. You can follow up with a letter or fax. To find out who represents you, visit www.lwv.org or call your local League of Women Voters office.

- ☼ Meet with elected officials. This is your right as a citizen, and it will be educational and empowering for your children. You might lobby the members of the city council, state legislature, or Congress for legislation in support of your cause. (Remember that national officials also have local offices where you can meet them.) Make an appointment with the secretary or scheduler and explain the purpose of your visit. Be informed and have a clear agenda before the meeting. Let your representative know what your family is willing to do in support of the bill or issue; for example, help draft legislation, give testimony, or contact other officials. Let them know what you hope they might do. Explain why the issue is relevant and important to their constituents. Keep your time together short and focused. Be sure to follow up on any agreements after the meeting and write a thank-you note reviewing the highlights of the meeting.

- ☼ Involve the media. Just because your issue is important doesn't mean it will be picked up by the media. You need to make it newsworthy by creating a catchy angle. Family involvement in any cause can be a great "hook." It's best to contact local magazines, newspapers, radio and TV stations when there will be a public event, a new project or campaign, or when you need public attention to accomplish your objectives.

- ☼ Create a newsletter. Newsletters help educate both your family and others. Think about whether this is an effective and efficient way to distribute information about your cause. Who would receive the newsletter? What would it include? Is your whole family willing to contribute? Start small and then grow as time, money, and needs increase.

- ☼ Start or sign a petition. Petitions indicate the kind of support you have for your cause and can bring your cause recognition. When designing your petition, get informed and then be specific about what you're asking for. Include a title, identify both who will receive and who has produced the petition, state the problem and how it can be resolved, collect signatures, and present your petition.

- ☼ Write letters to the editor. Thousands of people read the paper each day. What better way for your family to get your position heard? Have your family compose the letter together. Make it legible, brief, respectful, and informed. It is more likely to be published if it is relevant to a current issue or news item. Or have a letter-writing party. Get a group of families together to write letters to the editor and to elected officials in support of your cause.

BECOME A FAMILY OF ONLINE ACTIVISTS

It's easy to take action on a variety of critical issues by checking out the websites below. These sites describe current legislation or issues and tell you exactly how to make your voice heard. Perhaps your family could plan to meet once each month and decide which issues you want to respond to. Another possibility: Check out www.progressivesecretary.org, a service that will write letters, in your name, on selected issues.

Alliance to Save Energy
www.ase.org
Contact legislators about energy efficiency issues.

Amnesty International
www.aiusa.org
You can help free prisoners of conscience and work for human rights.

Bread for the World
www.bread.org
Its "offering of letters campaign" works to influence public policy in support of poor people.

CorpWatch
www.corpwatch.org
You can help keep corporations ethical by taking action on the latest campaigns.

Earth Island Institute
www.earthisland.org
Lets you respond to environmentally related action alerts.

Food First
www.foodfirst.org
Learn about actions that get at the roots of hunger and poverty.

The International Labor Rights Fund
www.laborrights.org
This site posts urgent action appeals in support of international labor rights.

League of Women Voters
www.lwv.org
Learn how to call or write letters to legislators in support of the League's main issues, including campaign finance and electoral reform.

National Coalition for the Homeless
www.nationalhomeless.org/alerts.html
Lets you respond to "legislative alerts" to help end homelessness.

National Wildlife Federation
www.nwf.org
You can help protect wildlife and wild places by responding to action alerts.

Oxfam
www.oxfamamerica.org
Help find solutions to hunger, poverty, and social injustice.

Physicians for Social Responsibility
www.psr.org
Respond to action alerts in support of peace, nuclear disarmament, and environmental health.

activism

☼ Develop a public service announcement (PSA). Your family can create its own PSA for the newspaper, radio, or television. First, ask for any PSA guidelines. Audio or video ads usually run 15, 30, or 60 seconds. For radio and TV, find out whether the ad should be written or recorded.

☼ Give a speech. Make it known that your family is available to give presentations on your issue. You might speak at schools, community centers, organizations, or public events. For tips on successfully writing and delivering speeches, read the section on public speaking in Marc and Craig Kielburger's book, *Take Action: A Guide to Active Citizenship,* (Toronto: Gage Learning, 2002).

☼ Organize a forum to educate others and increase awareness of an issue. A forum is a place for an open exchange of views on an issue. As the hosts, you don't need to be experts yourselves, but you must be informed enough to be able to invite knowledgeable participants. Hold the forum in a school or community center.

☼ Organize a boycott. This is a way to vote with your dollars. Business executives surveyed feel a boycott can be more effective than letter writing or lobbying, because of both the lost revenue and negative publicity. Learn more about current boycotts and how to organize your own by reading Co-op America's "Boycott Organizer's Guide" online (also see Chapter 10 for more information on boycotts).

www.boycotts.org

☼ Organize or attend a public demonstration. This can take the form of a march, vigil, rally, picket line, or sit-in. Your family can organize a demonstration in support of something or against it. Demonstrations can bring attention to or rally support for a cause or against an injustice, or seek to bring about practical changes. Plan it carefully and choose your timing to have the greatest impact. Decide whether to include speeches or a symbolic act of some kind. Read chapter 8 of Danny Seo's *Generation React* (New York: Bantam Books, 1997) for tips on organizing a protest.

☼ Create a website. Want to get your voice heard? What better way than to create your own web page. Whatever issue you choose, your family could be an online resource for information and education. Take turns doing research to keep it up to date.

Resources for Fighting for a Cause

Books for Kids

Generation Fix by Elizabeth Rusch (Hillsboro, OR: Beyond Words Publishing, 2002). Young adult. A series of inspiring stories of young people who have made a difference. These preteens and teens raised money for school supplies for needy children, testified against a ban on gay marriage, collected boxes of cereal for the hungry, and initiated a variety of other community service and social action projects.

Generation React: Activism for Beginners by Danny Seo (New York: Ballantine Books, 1997). Young adult. A highly readable guide with simple, practical tips for teens and adults who are interested in becoming activists.

Just Add Consciousness: A Guide to Social Activism by Oxfam America. Young adult and adult. This practical how-to manual is available online (free of charge), or you can order a copy from Oxfam America. You'll learn letter-writing techniques, how to meet with your congressperson, effective ways to use the media, and tips on organizing a demonstration.

Oxfam America
www.oxfamamerica.org
800-77-OXFAM (800-776-9326)
26 West Street, Boston, MA 02111

The Kid's Guide to Social Action: How to Solve the Social Problems You Choose—And Turn Creative Thinking Into Positive Action by Barbara A. Lewis (Minneapolis: Free Spirit Publishing, 1998). Young adult. The stories of kids who've made a difference will inspire young activists, and the how-to sections (on writing letters, creating petitions, fundraising, getting media coverage and more) will give kids and adults the skills they need to change the world.

People Power: A Look at Nonviolent Action and Defense by Susan Neiburg Terkel (New York: Penguin Books, 1996). Young adult. A primer on the use of nonviolence as a strategy for social change. Readers learn the true meaning of nonviolence, the history and success of nonviolent movements, and methods for putting the principles of nonviolence into practice.

Take Action: A Guide to Active Citizenship by Marc and Craig Kielburger (Toronto: Gage Learning Corporation, 2002). Young adult. Learn the practical tools you'll need to take action on issues that matter, including raising funds and awareness, writing petitions, surveys, and letters, using the media, and holding meetings.

Youth: The 26% Solution by Wendy Schaetzel Lesko and Emanuel Tsourounis (Kensington, MD: Activism 2000 Project, 1998). Young adult. Advice and strategies for taking action, influencing decision-makers, and using the press.

Organizations and Websites

20/20 Vision
www.2020vision.org
This site makes activism simple by supplying information on progressive causes and specific actions to take in support. Provides "tips for enhancing your political voice," including writing and calling elected officials, influencing editorials, and calling talk shows.

Community Toolbox
http://ctb.lsi.ukans.edu

A practical and comprehensive resource for the beginning activist. Covers everything from lobbying to demonstrating.

Youth Action Net
www.youthactionnet.org

The online toolkit provides tips on developing an advocacy strategy, fundraising, lobbying and writing proposals. A useful how-to guide for beginning activists.

Organize a Fundraiser

If you've ever stopped to buy a lemonade from a kid-run enterprise or purchased a 25-cent ticket to a neighborhood carnival, you know that kids can be unabashed entrepreneurs. Your family can harness that enthusiasm for money-making by sponsoring a fundraiser, with the proceeds going to the charity of your family's choice. And the nice thing about fundraising events is that while you're raising money, you can also educate people about the cause, build community, and have a lot of fun.

If possible, match the event with the goals of the organization. So, a carnival might be a good idea if you're raising money for a children's charity. A vegetable or flower sale would suit an environmental cause. A run or jump-a-thon might work for a health-related cause. Here are just a few ideas for fundraising events your family can organize.

Ideas for Fundraising

- Community carnival. You might include carnival rides, game booths, a bike or pet parade, food vendors and entertainment.

- Car wash. Find a spot that's easy to see from the street. Make large signs to advertise your price and the cause. Gather supplies, such as rags, buckets, dish soap and sponges. (Make certain there's a nearby water spigot.)

- Sell drinks. It can be lemonade, or buy soft drinks in bulk and sell it wherever hot, thirsty people gather.

- Babysit. Be available to babysit the neighborhood children one night each week and donate the money to your favorite charity.

- Craft sale. Ask talented family members and friends to donate items they've made.

- Children's talent show. Get the neighborhood kids together to strut their stuff. Rehearse, create programs and then charge admission.

- Bake sale. These are often best planned around another event. It will mean more customers. Consider asking a local bakery to donate goods.

☼ Vegetable or flower sale. Grow your own flowers or vegetables, sell them, and donate the proceeds.

☼ Candy sale. There are companies that provide candy for fundraisers, but they often keep a chunk of the money raised. If you have the money upfront, you can buy candy yourself from a wholesale store or you can ask stores or companies to donate for the cause. Then resell it at a profit.

TIPS FOR A SUCCESSFUL FUNDRAISER

Whether you're raising money for an animal shelter or a school playground, one strategy is to simply take up a collection. Often people are willing to donate to a good cause if asked. But if you'd prefer to organize an event, here are steps for arranging a successful fundraiser.

1. Brainstorm fundraising ideas and determine which event will be the most fun, effective and doable. (You can check out the choices above or come up with your own. Visit www.youthnoise.org to compare and contrast the costs and benefits of a variety of fundraisers.)
2. Make a timeline and a list of tasks that need to be accomplished. Make certain you have the time, resources and energy to organize the event.
3. Gather the supplies and equipment you'll need.
4. Create a budget. What will your expenditures be? How much do you expect to raise?
5. Determine the venue. Again make sure it fits with the fundraiser and is accessible enough to draw a crowd.
6. Advertise the event. Promotion might include invitations, flyers, tickets or banners; newsletters of community, churches or other organizations; neighborhood bulletin boards or a newspaper's community calendar.
7. Keep it fun. Remember that enthusiasm is the key to success.

fundraising

☼ Yard or garage sale. Ask for donations from friends, neighbors and community members. Remember, it will take time to collect, price and sell the items. And there may be a fee for advertising in the local paper. You can also put up signs around the neighborhood.

☼ Rent your family for chores. Offer your services for shoveling snow, raking leaves, cleaning, painting or other odd jobs. Let the recipients know that the proceeds will benefit charity.

☼ Raffle off something of value. Sell people a chance to win a prize. Remember, the more the prize is worth, the more people will be willing to pay for tickets. Try asking a local business to donate goods or services.

☼ Collect pennies. Visit www.pennies.org and click on "Penny Fundraisers."

☼ Give a party. Get a volunteer band and have someone donate food and drinks. Charge a small price for admission.

☼ Any A-Thons: Enlist pledges for whatever "a-thon" you can think of. Have people bike, walk, hop, jump, swim or skate. You could also rock in rocking chairs, dance, or read.

Resources for Fundraising

Books for Kids

Busy O'Brien and the Great Bubble Gum Blowout by Michelle Poploff, illustrated by Abby Carter (New York: Walker and Company, 1990). Ages 9-12. This out-of-print book (find it at your library) tells the story of kids trying to raise money for the local meals-on-wheels program.

Kid Cash: Creative Money-Making Ideas by Joe Lamancusa (Blue Ridge Summit, PA: TAB Books, 1999). Ages 9-12. A collection of projects that will encourage kids to earn some money—perhaps for charity. From the traditional to the creative.

Welcome to Starvation Lake by Gloria Whelan (New York: Golden Books, 2000). Ages 9-12. A group of fourth graders entices a rock band to play a concert to benefit the school library.

Generation React: Activism for Beginners by Danny Seo (New York: Ballantine Books, 1997). Young adult. Seo has fundraising down to an art form. Read Chapter 2 ("Super Easy Fund-Raising") before starting a project. He has ideas that will save you time and earn you bigger bucks.

Organizations and Websites

Youth Noise
www.youthnoise.org

This site provides a chart of various fundraisers and what you can expect in terms of staffing, time, complexity and earning power. Helpful for deciding which fundraiser might be most effective for your purposes. It also provides specific information on planning a variety of fundraisers. (Click on "Take Action" and then "Raise it and Donate it.")

Work for Human Rights, Peace, and Social Justice

On December 10, 1948, the United Nations General Assembly ratified the Universal Declaration of Human Rights (www.unhchr.ch/udhr/), which states that "equal and inalienable rights of all members of the human family is the foundation of freedom, justice and peace in the world." According to the Office of High Commissioner for Human Rights, the Declaration is now distributed in more than 300 languages and dialects, and it has become the most translated document in the world. But events around the world have made it clear that the eloquent principles expressed in the declaration are too often not applied.

Your family can take action in support of the principles of the declaration and help ensure dignity and equal treatment for people here and around the world by becoming advocates for human rights and social justice. You can join a human rights group, write letters of support for prisoners of conscience, or educate others about tolerance and justice.

Ideas for Working for Human Rights, Peace, and Social Justice

☼ Join Amnesty International. Your first step can be to join this well-respected human rights group. As a member, you can:

- Log on to the website and take immediate action by writing an e-mail to protest the treatment of a prisoner of conscience. Also, let legislators know how you feel about human rights issues.

- Join the Human Rights Action Center. You will receive e-mail alerts of human rights abuses along with a sample letter you can customize and send to the appropriate official.

- Join an activist group in your area. These groups work for particular prisoners of conscience they've "adopted." (Contact your regional office for more information.)

- Join the Freedom Writers Network. Write three letters each month in support of prisoners of conscience. (Samples are provided. You can edit those or compose your own.)

- Teach your kids about human rights and give them an opportunity to take action by visiting the Amnesty International web page designed specifically for children.

   Amnesty International
   www.aiusa.org/aikids/ (Kids)
   www.aiusa.org (United States)
   www.amnesty.org (International)
   212-807-8400
   322 Eighth Avenue, New York, NY 10001

☼ Take action in support of civil rights. Find out about current issues (including affirmative action, hate crimes, and religious freedom), or find civil rights groups in your area and learn how you can help.

www.civilrights.org

☼ Join Human Rights Watch (HRW). HRW researches and exposes human rights violations and pressures governments to support human rights. Take action on any number of its campaigns. The website contains information on specific issues or countries that may interest your family.

Human Rights Watch
www.hrw.org
212-290-4700
350 Fifth Avenue, 34th floor, New York, NY 10118-3299

☼ Campaign to ban landmines. The International Campaign to Ban Landmines is working to eliminate the use of landmines, support a treaty to ban landmines, and increase resources for victims.

International Campaign to Ban Landmines
www.icbl.org

☼ Work on human rights and tolerance at your child's school.

● Start an International Fair. Include speakers from around the world, performers of native dances and music, booths with food and games, or a fashion show with clothes from

IT'S A FAMILY AFFAIR

Everyone has a job when the Glaser-Leder family hosts the monthly membership committee of Rainbow Families, a resource and support group for lesbian, gay, bisexual, and transgender parents and their children. Greg Leder, along with his partner, Tom Glaser, and the five or six other committee members take care of the organization's membership paperwork. Leder and Glaser's son, 5-year-old Elliot, entertain the members' children. Elliot picks out the snack they'll serve, and helps organize the kids for activities, games, or a video. "It's helped Elliot learn how to share and how to lead, and these kids are now some of Elliot's best friends," says Leder. "Being around other kids with same-sex parents has been very valuable."

volunteering

different regions of the world. Guests might speak to the students about holidays, arts and crafts of their country, native animals, and their languages.

- Invite a speaker who can talk to the students about human rights.

- Publish a multicultural newsletter that promotes tolerance and diversity.

- Adopt a "partner" school, so that students of different backgrounds can get to know one another.

- Advocate for cultural diversity in the music program, theater productions, school speakers, and books used in classes. Donate materials related to human rights and tolerance to the school.

- Find many more ways to make a difference by checking out the school ideas in "101 Tools for Tolerance" at www.tolerance.org.

☼ Become a fair housing tester. Volunteers are trained to visit different places to inquire about housing in order to determine if discrimination is occurring. (For example, a white family and a black family may both visit a home to determine if they were treated equally.) Call your state human rights commission or local NAACP to ask about this opportunity.

☼ Help end discrimination against individuals with disabilities. If you notice places in your community that are not wheelchair accessible, bring them to the attention of the mayor's office and help ensure that action is taken.

☼ Support religious tolerance. Share information with others on a particular religion by making a presentation to your church, temple or synagogue. Also, explain the dangers of religious intolerance. Your family could also encourage a partnership between your church, temple, or synagogue and another faith community. Organize an interfaith youth group, or invite a clergy member of a different faith to address your congregation. The more we know about others, the less likely we are to be frightened of their beliefs.

☼ Take action for the rights of gays and lesbians. For information on current issues and how to make a difference, contact the American Civil Liberties Union, a group dedicated to supporting civil liberties, or the National Gay and Lesbian Task Force.

American Civil Liberties Union
www.aclu.org
125 Broad Street, 18th Floor, New York, NY 10004

National Gay and Lesbian Task Force
www.ngltf.org
202-393-5177
1325 Massachusetts Avenue NW, Suite 600, Washington, DC 20005

☼ The Southern Poverty Law Center estimates that 50,000 hate crimes occur in the United States each year. Do your part to make sure every such crime is counted, because "accurate collection of hate crime data will equip communities with the information necessary to shape effective strategies to deal with and prevent hate crimes." To find out what you can do, contact the Southern Poverty Law Center. You can receive a "Citizen's Action Kit" with information to combat intolerance, help monitor hate crimes through the group's Intelligence Project, and contribute your ideas on ways to fight hate.

Southern Poverty Law Center
www.splcenter.org
334-956-8200
400 Washington Avenue, Montgomery, AL 36104

☼ Work for children's rights.

● Push for adoption of the Convention on the Rights of the Child (CRC). Somalia (which has no central government) and the United States are the only two member nations of the United Nations who have not ratified this treaty. Also, campaign to encourage all countries to adopt the "optional protocol" of the CRC, which bans the use of child soldiers.

Human Rights Watch
www.hrw.org/children/

Child Rights Information Network
www.crin.org

Global Movement for Children
www.gmfc.org

Unicef
www.unicef.org/crc

● Join the Children's Defense Fund or the Child Welfare League of America. Both organizations promote the well being of children through education, services, research, and advocacy.

Child Welfare League of America
www.cwla.org
202-638-2952
440 First Street, NW, Third Floor, Washington, DC 20001

Children's Defense Fund
www.childrensdefense.org
202-628-8787
25 E Street, NW, Washington DC 20001

☼ Support the rights of women. Discrimination and violence against women are worldwide problems. Encourage your senators to have the United States ratify the Convention to Eliminate Discrimination Against Women (CEDAW).

United Nations' Division for the Advancement of Women
www.un.org/womenwatch/daw

Resources for Working for Human Rights, Peace, and Social Justice

Books for Kids

Amazing Grace by Mary Hoffman, illustrated by Caroline Binch (New York: Dial Books for Young Readers, 1991). Ages 4-8. A young girl named Grace decides she can be anything she wants to be. A beautiful story.

Different Just Like Me by Lori Mitchell (Watertown, MA: Charlesbridge Publishing, Inc., 1999). Ages 4-8. A young girl notices all the different ways people look, move around, and communicate. And she realizes how much we're all alike.

For Every Child by Caroline Castle (New York: Phyllis Fogelman Books, 2001). Ages 4-8. Using simple text and illustrations from acclaimed artists, this book portrays 14 of the principles of the U.N. Convention on the Rights of the Child.

Martin's Big Words: The Life of Dr. Martin Luther King by Doreen Rappoport, illustrated by Bryan Collier (New York: Hyperion Press, 2001). Ages 4-8. A simple introduction to the philosophy and words of Dr. King.

Mrs. Katz and Tush by Patricia Polacco (New York: Bantam Books, 1994). Ages 4-8. The touching story of an African-American boy and an older Jewish woman who share friendship and stories as they care for a kitten named Tush.

The Christmas Menorahs: How a Town Fought Hate by Janice Cohn, illustrations by Bill Farnsworth (Morton Grove, IL: Albert Whitman & Co., 1995). Ages 9-12. An inspiring story, based on real events, about the courage of one Montana town in the face of hate and intolerance.

The Civil Rights Movement for Kids by Mary Turck (Chicago: Chicago Review Press, 2000). Ages 9-12. Children learn about the history of the civil rights movement through songs, stories, activities, and photographs.

Irrepressible Spirit: Conversations with Human Rights Activists by Susan Kuklin (New York: G.P. Putnam's Sons, 1996). Young adult. Powerful interviews with courageous people who are fighting for human rights. The stories are searing, but the message is hopeful.

Stand Up, Speak Out: A Book About Children's Rights (London: Two-Can Publishing, 2001). Young adult. An examination of the U.N. Convention on the Rights of the Child through the drawings and writings of young people around the world.

Books for Parents

Speak Truth to Power: Human Rights Defenders Who Are Changing Our World by Kerry Kennedy Cuomo, photographs by Eddie Adams (New York: Crown Publishers, 2000). Portraits and interviews of human rights advocates from around the world. Look at this book with your children so they might know the true meaning of the word "hero."

We Can All Get Along: 50 Steps You Can Take to Help End Racism by Clyde W. Ford (New York: Dell Publishing, 1994). Learn specific actions you and your family can take to end the scourge of racism, both locally and around the world.

Organizations and Websites

Human Rights Web
www.hrweb.org
Learn about human rights, look at seminal documents in the history of human rights and read "Getting Started: A Primer for Beginning Human Rights Activists."

The Institute for Peace and Justice
www.ipj-ppj.org
314-533-4445
4144 Lindell Blvd., St. Louis, MO 63108
Learn about the Pledge of Nonviolence, the Parenting for Peace and Justice Network, and other campaigns of this interfaith nonprofit dedicated to working for peace and economic and social justice.

Kids Meeting Kids
www.kidsmeetingkids.org
212-662-2327
380 Riverside Drive, Box 8H, New York, NY 10025
Helps kids of different racial and ethnic groups get to know one another. The website has many ideas about how kids can make a difference, such as becoming pen pals with children from other countries, helping distribute petitions on children's rights, and making posters.

Universal Declaration of Human Rights
Franklin and Eleanor Roosevelt Institute
www.udhr.org

If you want to take action for human rights, there's no better place to learn exactly what needs to be done in the areas of women's and children's rights, halting religious persecution, and other issues.

Start a Grassroots Organization

When Annie Wignall of Newton, Iowa, was 11 years old, she founded an organization to pack "care bags" for kids in crisis. Her Care Bags Foundation now distributes the bags (filled with both fun and essential items, such as card games and toothbrushes) to more than 800 children each year. What made it such a success? Annie's mom, Cathy Wignall, offers this advice for people wanting to start a project: "Find something you have a passion for—Annie's passion is children—and do it simply for the pure joy of helping others. It will not only enrich other people's lives, but will enrich your own lives as well."

If your family is intrigued by keeping your local river clean, advocating for affordable housing, or starting a peer mediation program in your neighborhood school, one way to accomplish your dream is to establish your own organization. This can be both rewarding and exhilarating, and what better way to really get to know your family members than by undertaking a large project together? However, be certain you have the time and energy it will require. If you do, here are 10 steps to take for beginning a grassroots organization.

1. **Determine whether launching a new organization is necessary.** If an organization is already working on the goals your family has identified, join the group and simply add your efforts. You might also consider starting a local affiliate or chapter of a national organization. That will give you the advantage of name recognition and possibly some additional resources. If you can't find an existing organization with your specific focus, but there is one that is a close fit, discuss the possibility of adding your mission to its current mission. If this isn't feasible, it may be time to establish your own group.

2. **Create a mission statement.** Write out a succinct and carefully crafted sentence or two describing exactly what your organization exists to do. Include the name you have created. Use your mission statement when you explain your organization to others, and print it on any press releases, flyers, and brochures. To view mission statements of other organizations and better understand how to write your own, visit www.nonprofits.org/npofaq/03/21.html.

3. **Decide on specific goals and projects.** What actions do you have planned? What needs to happen to make the changes you envision? Once your organization has a mission, it's important to have concrete ideas about how to accomplish your goals. Determine specific, doable objectives for the first year. Ask yourself whether your plans are achievable and consistent with your mission. Some possibilities: Organize a letter-writing campaign, circulate a petition, hold an awareness rally, lobby for legislation, or organize a fundraising event. Network with members of other similar groups to learn about their own successes and failures, what works and what doesn't.

4. **Attract members.** Perhaps you'd like to invite other families to join you. You may want to keep it relatively small (some friends and family) at first and then open it to a more diverse membership. To attract new members, ask current members to invite friends, write an op-ed piece for your local paper, or hold an awareness rally. You might advertise in local media or distribute flyers. Remember that more members can mean a broader base of support and more clout.

5. **Arrange a meeting place and time.** Find a venue that is free, easily accessible, and able to accommodate the number of people you plan to include. Perhaps you'd like to establish monthly meetings so your members can stay involved, but not be overwhelmed. Always have an agenda to keep the meeting focused. Offering food can help attract new people!

6. **Establish the organizational hierarchy and decision-making process.** Who will be the leader? Will you have officers? Will you establish committees with different responsibilities? How will decisions be made—by consensus or by vote? You might consider alternating the person (or family) who will lead each meeting.

7. **Decide on a budget and funding sources.** First, determine what you'll need for operating expenses in the first year. How exactly will your money be spent? Who will decide on fiscal matters? Then, consider how you will raise funds: Ask for donations, organize a fundraising event, or apply for a grant?

8. **Generate publicity for your organization and its goals.** Use leaflets, posters, press releases, op-ed pieces, and rallies. (Make certain you can handle inquiries generated from your media campaign. Otherwise, hold off until you're more organized.)

9. **Have fun.** Especially when there are children involved, it's important to keep the activities enjoyable. If you get too stressed, too serious, or too overwhelmed, then the primary benefit of working together as a family has been lost. Enjoy your events, celebrate your victories, and encourage one another.

10. **Incorporate and apply for nonprofit status.** Incorporating and filing for nonprofit status enables you to more easily apply for grants, receive tax-deductible contributions, and reduce personal liability. How you do this varies from state to state. Get more information on how to proceed from the Foundation Center or

contact your local bar association to find an attorney who does work with nonprofit organizations.

The Foundation Center
Establishing a Nonprofit Organization
www.fdncenter.org/learn/classroom/establish
212- 620-4230
79 Fifth Avenue, New York, NY 10003

Resources for Starting a Grassroots Organization

Books for Kids

Generation React: Activism for Beginners by Danny Seo (New York: Ballantine Books, 1997). Young adult. Check out the first chapter, "Organization 101," on starting your own group.

Take Action: A Guide to Active Citizenship by Marc and Craig Kielburger (Toronto: Gage Learning Corporation, 2002). Young adult. Practical information on building a team to fight for your cause, making a plan of action, and calling meetings.

Organizations and Websites

Charity Focus
www.charityfocus.org

Internet Nonprofit Center
The Nonprofit FAQ
http://nonprofits.org/npofaq

Nonprofit Charitable Organizations
http://nonprofit.about.com/mbody.htm

Nonprofit Genie
www.genie.org

Volunteer Vacations 8

Here's how 14-year-old Sarah Ingebritsen of Spokane, Washington, spent one summer vacation: She woke each morning at 6 a.m. to the sound of roosters crowing and the glare of the morning sun in the large dorm room she shared with her 10-year-old sister, Kim Ingebritsen, her parents, Joe Chrastil and Jean Ingebritsen, and the other volunteers at the Jubilee House Community in Nueva Vida, Nicaragua (see page 157)—a refugee settlement of 12,000 people who lost their homes during Hurricane Mitch. Sarah got dressed, waited in line for the bathroom, and helped herself to some breakfast of toast and peanut butter or leftover rice and beans. Just before 9 a.m. she rode in the back of a pick-up truck to the free local pharmacy where she helped fill prescriptions, stock shelves, and serve patients. She had lunch with the other volunteers, then worked again until 5. The rest of her family spent the day helping to construct a new health clinic. After a communal dinner, the family played cards, read, journaled, and talked until bedtime. "It was hard being away from my friends," says Sarah, "but it felt so good to know I was helping out and making a difference in people's lives. It's changed me forever."

Like this family, an increasing number of travelers are choosing volunteering as a rewarding way of seeing the world. Most service-oriented vacations don't require participants to have any specific skills—just enthusiasm, open-mindedness, and a willingness to pay their own expenses (ranging up to several thousand dollars per person). And there are all kinds of volunteer options—maintaining trails, working with children, or building and renovating houses, schools, and community centers. There truly is something for everyone.

The Volunteer Vacation

Sure, relaxing on the beach is fun, but with volunteer travel you come home with more than just good photos and a tan. Volunteer travel lets you make a contribution to the larger community. Dozens of organizations, here and abroad, depend on vacation volunteers to help with environmental projects, educate disadvantaged children, and do construction work. For example, you can travel to Xi'an, China, to teach English to children and young adults or to Yosemite to plant oak trees and rebuild trails. And although the work is often hard, you almost always have an opportunity to sightsee, relax, and enjoy local activities.

If you choose an international volunteer vacation, your family will truly become part of another culture by living and working with local people. That gives you an opportunity to learn from others in a way that traditional tourists never experience. This is especially true if the volunteers hail from varying countries. "Our volunteers get to know a community and its people on a new level—as an invited guest, not only as a tourist," says Barb DeGroot, Senior Writer for Global Volunteers, an organization that sponsors volunteer travel opportunities.

Volunteer travel can sometimes cost less than a traditional vacation and is often tax deductible. But it is not necessarily cheap. The organizations sponsoring these programs usually don't have the resources to provide transportation, food, or lodging for volunteers. But most participants feel that they get more than they give. They cite the pleasure of having their family spend an extended time together—from a few days to several months—sharing something meaningful. Also, kids of all ages benefit from the responsibility they're given and from being treated as a member of a team. "There is no greater classroom than the world for kids with eager minds. And what a wonderful way to teach our children the true joy of service to others," says DeGroot. And for those who can't volunteer regularly at home due to heavy work schedules and other responsibilities, volunteer travel provides a chance to contribute while spending time with family and enjoying a break from routine.

Choosing the Right Project

Take time to choose the volunteer project that's right for your family. Request information from a number or organizations. (You might also check with your church, temple, or synagogue about community service trips.) Then speak with the program coordinator about your family—the ages of your children, any special skills or interests, and what you want to gain from your experience. Consider these questions before deciding:

☼ What projects will you be working on? What are the responsibilities? What are the working conditions? Is the work very physical? What will your children be assigned to do? Will the family be working together?

☼ How many volunteers will there be? Do they understand that children will be part of the team?

☼ How much time does the program expect you to commit? Programs can last anywhere from a weekend to several months. Consider what you can spare and how long your children will want to be away from home.

☼ What are the accommodations? Are you responsible for finding your own place to stay? Will you be living with a local family? Will your family members all be housed together? Is there running water and electricity? What type of food is available? In some cases the volunteers help cook. Other times a cook may accompany the group, or you'll eat in local restaurants or be served by local people. Think about how well your children will be able to adjust to a new diet.

☼ Is there a minimum or maximum age for volunteers? Some programs only take children over 12 or over 16.

☼ Is there enough leisure time? Are there recreational opportunities? Is there an opportunity for additional travel? It may be important to consider what kid-friendly entertainment is nearby. During your downtime, your kids will need an outlet. Some sites may be remote and lacking in cultural activities.

☼ What is the cost? Be certain you understand what is included in the fee. Note that transportation is often additional. It's helpful to shop around to find the programs that are the most economical. Think also about whether you're interested in purchasing travel insurance. You might consider holding a fundraiser to meet your expenses.

☼ Are there suitable medical facilities? Is accident insurance provided? What happens if you or your child becomes ill or someone gets hurt? Is someone on the team trained in first aid? If you're considering a trip to a developing country, speak to your child's pediatrician and your own physician beforehand. And do so as early in the process as possible. (If immunizations are required, some may need to be taken in a series over a period of time.) Finally, bring your doctor's phone number with you when you travel in case you have additional questions or concerns. (Visit the Centers for Disease Control and Prevention at www.cdc.gov and the International Association for Medical Assistance to Travellers at www.iamat.org for additional health-related information.)

☼ What kind of orientation is offered? Is training or instruction provided?

☼ Does the program have a religious affiliation?

☼ How far in advance must you apply for the program? Some recommend six weeks, others need volunteers lined up six months in advance.

☼ Does the program typically include families as volunteers? Will you have an opportunity in advance of the trip to speak with other families who have volunteered?

Preparing Your Family

Let your children know what to expect before you embark on your adventure. Talk often about where you'll be living and the kind of work you'll be doing. Describe the conditions and the food. Most programs will have orientation materials to help prepare you and your family.

If you're traveling abroad, learn about the country or culture you'll be experiencing. For example, a trip to Peru to help build a school is an excellent opportunity for your children to learn some Spanish and the history and geography of South America. The more educated all of you are before you go, the more you'll benefit.

Explain the rules of behavior to your children. This is particularly important if your family will be in a culture in which the rules of conduct are different from our own. This can be an important lesson for children in cultural dynamics.

Be enthusiastic. Describe the trip to your kids as an adventure of a lifetime (which it is), but also be realistic about the conditions you'll face. Then have a great time!

Resources for Volunteer Vacations

Books for Parents

How to Live Your Dream of Volunteering Overseas by Joseph Collins, Stefano DeZerega, and Zahara Heckscher (New York: Penguin Books, 2002). Everything you need to know about being an international volunteer, including organizational profiles, how to volunteer without an organized program, and how to pay for it. An index lists the organizations that accept families. www.volunteeroverseas.org.

Volunteer Vacations: Short-Term Adventures That Will Benefit You and Others by Bill McMillon, Doug Cutchins, and Anne Geissinger (Chicago: Chicago Review Press, 2003). A comprehensive guide to volunteer vacationing. Most of the opportunities McMillon discusses are not suitable for younger children, but he has scores of possibilities for families with teenagers.

Organizations and Websites

Action Without Borders: Organizations Promoting Volunteering
www.idealist.org/travel.html

This site lists dozens of organizations that sponsor volunteer vacations abroad and offers links to their websites. Take a tour and see what opportunities exist. You'll need to be selective, because these are not specifically for families.

Goabroad.com
www.goabroad.com

You'll find all you need to know about volunteering, working, or studying abroad. You can search for volunteer opportunities by country.

International Volunteer Programs Association
www.volunteerinternational.org

This site provides comprehensive information for anyone interested in volunteering abroad.

Peacework
www.peacework.org

This organization generally arranges volunteer trips for pre-established groups, but it also has openings for individual volunteers or families within these groups.

Service Leader: Guide to Volunteering Outdoors in Parks and Wilderness Areas
www.serviceleader.org

This site provides links to volunteer opportunities for outdoor enthusiasts. If this is your family's passion, you'll want to discover the possibilities. Click on "For Volunteers" and then on "Guide to Volunteering Outdoors in Parks and Wilderness Areas."

Volunteer Vacation Opportunities

GLOBAL VOLUNTEERS

375 E. Little Canada Road
St. Paul, MN 55117-1628
651-407-6100
800-487-1074
www.globalvolunteers.org
E-mail: email@globalvolunteers.org

Description: This nonprofit, nonsectarian organization sponsors work projects all over the world. Younger children (ages 5 to 10) are welcome at many of the U.S. sites, especially American Indian reservations, where they have the opportunity to interact with the local children. Global Volunteers has also hosted younger children in Costa Rica and Ecuador. Teens and children over 10 years of age would fit in well at Global Volunteer's summer English language camps, where volunteers teach English to young students in Italy, Greece, Poland, and China. These camps provide young volunteers the opportunity to befriend local youth. Mature older children or teens might consider working with babies in "failure to thrive" clinics in Romania, but this is a demanding, emotionally draining endeavor.

Where: China, the Cook Islands, Hungary, India, Ghana, Tanzania, Costa Rica, Ecuador, Ireland, Jamaica, Poland, Romania, Spain, Italy, Greece, Ukraine, and the United States

Type of Work: Volunteer opportunities might include teaching conversational English or business skills; feeding and caring for children; assisting with health care; building and repairing homes, schools and community centers; or assisting with natural resource projects.

Length: 1, 2, or 3 weeks

Cost: Prices range from $650 per person (not including airfare) for a program in the continental United States to $2,395 for three weeks in China (not including visa fee or airfare to Xi'an). There are children's fees available. The cost is tax-deductible.

Food and Lodging: Depending on the site, volunteers may stay in college dorm rooms, family homes, conference centers, hotel rooms, guesthouses, villas, or community buildings. Participants may eat the local food in their hotel or at restaurants, or eat meals prepared by volunteers or local cooks.

How to Apply: Call a volunteer coordinator for information and an application. Apply early because the trips fill up fast. A $350 deposit per person is required with your application to hold a spot. The balance is due 75 days before you're scheduled to arrive at your project destination. You can also apply online.

GLOBAL CITIZENS NETWORK

130 N. Howell Street
St. Paul, MN 55104
651-644-0960
800-644-9292
www.globalcitizens.org
E-mail: info@globalcitizens.org

Description: Volunteers from Global Citizens Network (GCN) work with local people on projects in rural areas around the world. This includes several Indian reservations. Most of GCN's programs are open to families. Volunteers are encouraged to become part of the community and take part in its daily rituals, which might include learning local dances or preparing native food. Evenings are spent talking with other volunteers about the day's events.

Where: Kenya, Guatemala, Nepal, Mexico, Peru, Tanzania, and Native American Reservations in Arizona and New Mexico

Type of Work: All projects are initiated and led by people in the local community and might include building or renovating a health clinic or youth center, teaching in a local elementary school, or planting trees.

Length: Trips can last 1, 2, or 3 weeks.

Cost: Prices range from $650 for trips inside the United States to $1,950 for the trips to Kenya, Tanzania, and Nepal. This includes food, lodging, in-country travel, a donation to the community project and a portion of the team leader's expenses. Children between the ages of 8 and 12 are half-price. Returning volunteers get a $50 discount. Airfare is not included. All costs are tax deductible.

Food and Lodging: Volunteers stay in local homes or in a community center. They eat meals with their host family, or eat food prepared by team members or a local cook.

How to Apply: Information and an application are available via phone or on the website. Volunteers need to submit a $200 deposit with their application to reserve a place. Be certain to get a confirmation before purchasing airline tickets.

CROSS CULTURAL SOLUTIONS

2 Clinton Place
New Rochelle, NY 10801
800-380-4777
914-632-0022
www.crossculturalsolutions.org
E-mail: info@crossculturalsolutions.org

Description: Cross Cultural Solutions pairs local grassroots organizations with small groups of volunteers from all over the world to work on community projects such as education, health care, and community development. The staff customizes the work for volunteers based on their interests and experience. Children must be at least 9 years of age. Evenings and weekends are reserved for leisure activities, including travel.

Where: India, Ghana, Peru, China, Russia, Thailand, Costa Rica, Brazil, Guatemala, and Tanzania

Type of Work: Volunteers are involved in community-based projects, such as caring for children in local orphanages, teaching arts and crafts, assisting health care workers, teaching English to adults and children, and teaching marketable skills to women.

Length: Between 2 and 12 weeks. Longer programs may be arranged.

Cost: Ranges from $1,985 for two weeks to $2,315 for three weeks. (Children under 13 receive a 50% discount.) The fee includes meals, accommodations, ground transportation, in-country staff, program, medical and emergency evacuation insurance, and administrative costs, but not airfare. Program fee and airfare are tax deductible.

Food and Lodging: Cross Cultural Solutions maintains homes or apartments in all areas where volunteers work. Meals are generally simple and consistent with local cuisine.

How to Apply: Volunteers can register online, by phone, or by mailing or faxing an application. The non-refundable registration fee of $275 is applied to the program fee.

SEEDS OF LEARNING

585 Fifth Street West
Sonoma, CA 95476
707-939-0471
www.seedsoflearning.org
E-mail: info@seedsoflearning.org

Description: The mission of Seeds of Learning (SOL) is to enhance educational opportunities in rural Latin America. SOL sponsors about 10 work groups a year with 10 to 18 volunteers in each. Most are between mid-April and mid-August. There are intergenerational camps for families and youth camps for teenagers and chaperones. Children under 16 years of age must travel with a parent or guardian. On weekends there are group outings to local attractions, and every afternoon is devoted to educational programs or field trips.

Where: Nicaragua, El Salvador, and Guatemala

Type of Work: Most work groups build part of a school, alongside members of the local community. This might involve digging, mixing cement, laying brick or block, and carrying water. Less strenuous work is available for young children and others who may request it. Some volunteers may spend time caring for and teaching local children.

Length: 10-day to 3-week programs

Cost: The rate is $900 per person for a 10-day trip, $950 for two weeks and $1,500 for the three-week trip, which includes a week of language study in Guatemala. The fee includes room and board, in-country transportation, and a donation for construction materials, but doesn't include airfare. The trip cost is tax deductible.

Food and Lodging: Volunteers stay in a hostel in Nicaragua, and in a hostel or hotel in El Salvador. Participants may prepare some meals themselves; others are catered by local families or restaurants.

How to Apply: For information or to apply, call, e-mail, or visit their website. Include your name, mailing address, phone number, and preferred dates and country.

CARIBBEAN VOLUNTEER EXPEDITIONS

Box 388
Corning, NY 14830
607-962-7846
www.cvexp.org
E-mail: ahershcve@aol.com

Description: This non-profit agency sponsors about eight trips per year with the goal of preserving and documenting the heritage of the Caribbean. (About half the trips are open to families.) Half the day is spent working; the other half is reserved for leisure activities like swimming, exploring, and relaxing. CVE warns volunteers to be ready for thorns, mosquitoes, and heat.

Where: Sites throughout the Caribbean

Type of Work: Volunteers work on historical preservation projects such as measuring and photographing historical structures, helping Caribbean agencies keep a record of local architecture, and gathering information on Caribbean history and architecture. Tasks might also include painting, minor carpentry, archaeology, and cemetery inventories.

Length: Usually 1 week

Cost: Ranges from $500 to $1,000 and includes room, board, and in-country transportation.

Food and Lodging: CVE arranges for volunteers to stay at a campsite, hotel, or guest house.

How to Apply: Call, write, or e-mail for further information and an application.

EXPLORATIONS IN TRAVEL

2458 River Road
Guilford, VT 05301
802-257-0152
www.exploretravel.com
E-mail: explore@volunteertravel.com

Description: Explorations in Travel works with volunteers from all over the world and arranges each placement individually in order to match participants with the most appropriate work. Language classes can also be included in the placement. The website lists current volunteer opportunities, which change continually as positions fill and others become available. Call to find out which programs are open to families.

Where: Puerto Rico, Mexico, Costa Rica, Guatemala, Ecuador, Belize, Australia, and Nepal

Type of Work: A variety of positions are available, including work in biological reserves, conservation areas, national parks and forests, schools, organic farms, and animal shelters.

Length: Each placement is arranged individually, so volunteers determine their own commitment time.

Cost: Placement fees range from $775 to $975, depending on the position. This does not include airfare or room and board. Lodging and food usually run $10 to $15 per day.

Food and Lodging: Explorations in Travel will arrange for food and lodging. Participants may live in a dormitory, bunkhouse, or with a host family.

How to Apply: Call or write for an application or apply online. There is a $35 nonrefundable application fee.

VOLUNTEERS FOR PEACE INTERNATIONAL WORKCAMPS

1034 Tiffany Road
Belmont, VT 05730
802-259-2759
www.vfp.org
E-mail: vfp@vfp.org

Description: Volunteers For Peace (VFP) sponsors more than 2,000 workcamps each year, but the vast majority are only for volunteers over 18. However, VFP does list about 20 family camps each year. Most occur between June and September, and participants are generally placed between April and June for summer and fall programs. A few opportunities are offered in the winter and spring. Volunteers at each site usually come from four or more countries, so this program is truly international.

Where: VFP has camps in more than 70 countries.

Type of Work: The work varies widely depending on which camp is selected. It might include construction and restoration of low-income housing or community buildings or environmental projects such as trail building, park maintenance, or organic farming. There are also social service projects such as working with children, the elderly, the physically or mentally handicapped, refugees, minority groups, and drug/alcohol recovery patients. Other types of work include historic preservation, archaeology, and AIDS education.

Length: Usually 2 to 3 weeks, but you can register for additional camps in the same or different countries to extend your trip.

Cost: You must pay a $20 membership to view the VFP directory of workcamps online and to participate. (Using your credit card, you can join via the website.) Most programs require a $200 registration fee, which includes room and board. Participants pay for their own transportation. Programs in Russia, Africa, and Latin America run $300 to $500.

Food and Lodging: Usually participants are housed in a school, church, private home, or community center. Living arrangements are cooperative, which means sharing accommodations, food preparations, and other chores.

How to Apply: After becoming a VFP member, you'll get a workcamp directory listing the programs, including those available to families. Members can print an application from the website, which can then be mailed back or faxed. Placements are made within five days of receiving the application. Register before mid-May for the best selection.

PASSPORT IN TIME (PIT)

P.O. Box 31315
Tucson, AZ 85751-1315
800-281-9176
520-722-2716
www.passportintime.com
E-mail: pit@sricrm.com

Description: Passport in Time, a volunteer program of the USDA Forest Service, coordinates volunteers to work on archaeological and historic preservation projects. Participants work with professionals who act as "hosts, guides, and coworkers." Some programs do not permit children under 18, but many include children if they are with a responsible adult. All projects are listed in the PIT newsletter, which can be ordered free of charge or is available online.

Where: National forests throughout the United States

Type of Work: Work might include archaeological excavation, rock art restoration, surveys, archival research, historic structure restoration, oral history research, or brochure writing.

Length: The commitment varies from two days to two weeks, but in some cases it's possible to stay longer.

Cost: There is no fee to participate, but sometimes families must cover their own food and lodging. Volunteers pay their own travel expenses.

Food and Lodging: Depending on the site, volunteers can camp, stay at local hotels, or use hookups for RVs. Food is sometimes prepared by a camp cook for a fee. Other times volunteers are responsible for their own meals.

How to Apply: Apply online, or fax or mail the application. You'll be notified of your acceptance about three weeks after the project application deadline.

SOUSSON FOUNDATION

3600 Ridge Road
Templeton, CA 93465
800-77-4-PARK
www.sousson.org
E-mail: info@sousson.org

Description: The Sousson Foundation, which promotes preservation and rehabilitation of the western national parks, encourages families with children 7 years and older to participate in any of their programs, most of which involve camping. Half the trip is devoted to volunteer conservation work, while the other half is spent hiking, rafting, snorkeling, or exploring the national parks. "We believe strongly in making family memories and traditions," says Mark Landon, director of the foundation. Sousson offers more than a dozen expeditions a year for up to 22 volunteers each.

Where: The western national parks, including the Channel Islands, Yosemite, Hawaii, the Sequoia and Kings Canyon, and the High Sierra

Type of Work: Conservation projects might involve building and restoring trails, planting trees or seedlings, building enclosures to protect threatened flora, or removing non-native vegetation.

Length: 6 to 8 days

Cost: The cost is between $595 and $985 per person, which includes meals, campsites, and camping equipment.

Food and Lodging: Food is usually prepared at the campsite by an outdoor gourmet chef. In Hawaii, participants stay in a lodge and eat some meals in restaurants.

How to Apply: Apply online or call for an application.

CENTER FOR DEVELOPMENT IN CENTRAL AMERICA

Jubilee House Community, Inc.
De Km.11 Carretera Nueva a Leon, 1.6 km. Abajo
Continguo Hacienda Masili, Ciudad Sandino
Managua, Nicaragua
Phone in Nicaragua: 011-505-883-6634
Phone messages in US: 1-800-ASHEVIL
www.jhc-cdca.org
E-mail: jhc@ns.sdnnic.org.ni

Description: The Jubilee House Community is a non-sectarian faith-based intentional community designed to assist impoverished communities in Nicaragua to become self sufficient through development work in five areas: health, education, sustainable agriculture, appropriate technology, and sustainable economic development. Five adults and three children who are based in Nicaragua serve as hosts for the volunteer delegations, which help with any work the local people believe is critical to their well-being. (No child care is provided.)

Where: Nicaragua

Type of Work: A variety of help is needed in the areas of health care, construction, agriculture, and computer work. Volunteers typically work the same hours as the Nicaraguans, 8 a.m. to 5 p.m., Monday through Friday (8 a.m. till noon on Saturday).

Length: Arranged individually

Cost: Each volunteer contributes $25 per day for room, board, and in-country transportation. (The cost goes down to $10 for those who volunteer for between one and three months and to $5 for volunteers who stay longer than three months.) Volunteers pay their own travel expenses.

Food and Lodging: Volunteers sleep on bunk beds in a large dorm room in Jubilee House. There is a communal kitchen, and volunteers help with cooking and cleanup.

How to Apply: No forms are necessary, but the Jubilee House Community asks that you write a letter describing your family, your interests and skills, and other information you think is important.

SCOTTIE'S PLACE

P.O. Box 905
Powell Mountain Road
Peterstown, WV 24963
800-621-5676
www.scottiesplace.org
E-mail: scottiesplace@usa.net

Description: Scottie's Place is a two-week summer camp for children who are experiencing homelessness, and also offers weekend and holiday programs throughout the year. Its mission is to empower, educate, and enliven homeless children. The camp provides children the opportunity to canoe, swim, hike, do crafts, care for animals, and participate in community service work. Volunteers who spend time working as camp counselors will need to submit to a background check.

Where: Peterstown, West Virginia

Type of Work: Volunteers build cabins and fences, clear trails, garden, do maintenance and repair work, help with mailings and correspondence, and solicit donations of items needed for the camp. Larger projects are done when campers are not present. If your family volunteers during a session, you'll spend most of your time interacting with the kids.

Length: The sessions last 2 weeks, but volunteers may come for 1 day or several months. Your family determines the length of stay.

Cost: Fees are determined on a case-by-case basis.

Food and Lodging: Conditions are rustic. Lodging is in a tent or Native American longhouse. Food is cooked in the communal kitchen and served outdoors.

How to Apply: Contact the camp at the address and phone number listed above.

Additional Opportunities for Families With Kids Over Age 12

HUDSON RIVER SLOOP CLEARWATER, INC.

112 Little Market Street
Poughkeepsie, NY 12601
845-454-7673
www.clearwater.org
E-mail: educator@clearwater.org

Description: This is an actual tall ship that provides environmental education programs for school groups, community organizations, camps, and adult groups. Between four and six volunteers are onboard throughout the sailing season (early April to early November) to help with education programs and boat maintenance. Children ages 12 to 15 must be accompanied by a parent or guardian. There are usually not more than two family members chosen for any one week, so only a parent/child team should apply.

Where: Hudson River

Type of Work: Volunteers assist crew in teaching, sailing, boat maintenance, and daily chores.

Length: 1 week

Cost: Plan to spend $45 on food per week. Membership dues in the Clearwater organization are required. Student dues are $15; individual dues are $35; a family membership is $50.

Food and Lodging: Volunteers eat and sleep on the boat.

How to Apply: Submit application 8 to 10 weeks before the dates you wish to volunteer. Volunteers will be notified 3 to 6 weeks in advance if they have been accepted. More people apply than are accepted in the summer months. Spring and fall dates may be more open.

Santa Catalina Island Conservancy

> P.O. Box 2739
> Avalon, CA 90704
> 310-510-2595, Ext. 109
> www.catalinaconservancy.org
> E-mail: volunteers@CatalinaConservancy.org

Description: This 76-square-mile island is an important habitat for rare and endangered plants and animals. Volunteers help protect the habitat and are expected to be in good physical condition. Workdays usually run from 8:30 a.m. until 3:30 p.m.

Where: Santa Catalina Island, less than 20 miles from Los Angeles

Type of Work: Volunteers do hands-on fieldwork for the preservation and restoration of the island landscape, including research and study of the waters surrounding the island. You may guide visitors on hikes, help in the native plant nursery, maintain trails, or monitor wildlife.

Length: 5 days

Cost: The $160 fee includes round-trip boat fare from either Long Beach, Newport Beach, or Dana Point; transfers between the town of Avalon and the island campsite; plus lodging, dinner, and membership in the Conservancy.

Food and Lodging: The Laura Stein Volunteer Camp, where participants are lodged, consists of two large tents with eight bunk beds in each. For more privacy, you can bring your own tent. There are bathroom facilities, running water, and an outdoor kitchen. Dinners are prepared by volunteer chefs. Volunteers are responsible for their own breakfast, lunch, and snacks.

How to Apply: Request an application by e-mail, phone or mail. You must include a $50 deposit with your application. Apply early because space is limited.

Amizade, LTD

920 William Pitt Union
Pittsburgh, PA 15260
888-973-4443
www.amizade.org
E-mail: volunteer@amizade.org

Description: This nonprofit group partners with local grassroots organizations to work on community development projects around the world. Each Amizade program provides volunteers with opportunities for community service, education, and recreation. For groups of six or more, Amizade will customize a program. Volunteers between 12 and 17 years of age are welcome at any of the project sites but must be accompanied by a parent or legal guardian.

Where: Brazil, Bolivia, Northern Ireland, Jamaica, Tanzania, Nepal, Australia, Greater Yellowstone Region in Montana, and Navajo Nation in Arizona

Types of Work: Volunteers may be involved in trail maintenance, tutoring, work in a tree nursery, historic restoration, or construction projects such as building a school playground or community center.

Length: 1 week to 1 year

Cost: Fees range from $475 for 1 week in Yellowstone to $1899 for 2 weeks in Nepal. This includes room and board, travel at the project site, all activities and materials, donation to the project site, plus staff and administrative fees. Families of four or more receive a discount. Travel to the program site, passports, visas, immunization, and departure taxes are not included in the fee. All costs are tax deductible.

Food and Lodging: Volunteers generally live together in dormitories, tents, or houses. Home stays can be arranged for longer programs. Meals are provided.

How to Apply: E-mail or call for an application or more information. Or download an application from the website. A deposit of $100 for U.S. programs and $350 for international programs is required with your application. Many programs fill up quickly.

Effective Ways to Support Your Family's Values and Beliefs 9

Volunteering is only one of the ways your family can live out your vision for a better world and teach your kids to be compassionate global citizens. It's also important to consider how we spend and donate our money. Every family—whether we shop at Saks Fifth Avenue or our neighborhood used clothing store—has dollar power. From choosing which charities are worthy of our support to deciding which brand of cereal to purchase, we influence programs and policies by what we choose do with our money. Here are some guidelines for helping your family donate to charities that are making a real difference in the community, shop with a conscience and support businesses with values you share, and donate unused or unwanted items that can be of use to someone else.

Give to Charity

In a Jewish folktale, a mysterious man magically blesses a poor farmer and his wife and children with riches for six years. The wife, Esther, suggests to her husband that they use the money to help others—buying shoes for a barefoot child and assisting a mother with her son's bar mitzvah. When the stranger appears six years later to reclaim the wealth, he finds it has been distributed throughout the community. It's clear that by sharing, the riches remain with the family always, and the thread of kindness they began "stretches on to this very day" (Shollar, 2000).

Teaching children about giving their time, money, or resources makes them rich with compassion and a sense of community responsibility, and begins a thread of generosity and kindness that can extend through the generations. And it's not just for the wealthy. A survey entitled, "Giving and Volunteering in the United States" conducted by the Independent Sector, found that 89% of all American families donate to charity, averaging 3.2% of their income (www.independentsector.org). In fact, families with lower incomes actually give away a larger percentage than wealthier ones. All of us have a responsibility to share with those in need, contribute to causes we believe in, and support the changes necessary to build a better world. Besides, giving is fun and it makes us feel good, no matter how much we can donate. Let your children share the joy. Here are some tips for making charitable giving a family affair.

Ideas for Giving to Charity

☼ Discuss charities and decisions about donations in a family meeting. When your children are young, talk about which causes are particularly important to you and why. Let them know how you determine the recipient and the amount of money to donate. Later, let them have input into the decision. Explain that some charities use their money more effectively and responsibly than others. One family saves charitable solicitations they receive, puts them in a box, and every few months they sit down together and decide who deserves their money. Another family divides the money they're donating among family members and has each person decide where to give their portion. Regardless of the strategy, it's important to begin early teaching about sharing and giving.

☼ Make your giving meaningful to your children. Choose organizations with missions and programs your child can relate to. For example, a preschooler will be thrilled to donate money to a local animal shelter, but may be confused about the purpose of Amnesty International. If the organization you support is local, visit with your children and see how your money is working. Or write for information and share it with the family. This will make the giving more real for you and your kids.

"Clearly, sharing one's own financial resources with others reinforces and shapes social values and can deepen a sense of meaning, purpose, and contribution. A commitment to giving can set young people on a life course toward being contributing members of society who see it as their responsibility to look out for the well-being of others. And, finally, a focus on giving can help to shift priorities into balance in a culture where the drive to accumulate wealth can consume or overwhelm all other aspects of life."

values

Source: *Growing Up Generous: Engaging Youth in Giving and Serving* by Eugene C. Roehlkepartain, Elanah Dalyah Naftali, and Laura Musegades (The Alban Institute, 2000)

☼ Encourage some sacrifice. Have each member of the family give up something in order to donate money to a charity you've agreed to support. For example, you might skip a dinner out or forgo your morning latte, then donate the savings. Your child might choose to give up candy or movies for a week or mow the neighbor's lawn to earn money for charity. The important thing is sacrificing something of personal value—either time or money—for the good of the community.

CHECKING OUT CHARITIES

How do you make an informed decision about where to give your money? How can you be certain that the charity you've chosen is ethical and that your donation is being used responsibly? Here are some issues to consider before investing your money to help others. And remember, never give out your credit card or bank information over the phone. Some experts also recommend never giving money to any organization that refuses to send written materials.

What is the charity's mission? How exactly will your dollars be spent? Call and ask questions about the charity's goals and successes.

Ask. Talk to people who know the field about the reputation of the organization.

Show up. Go to an activity or event the charity sponsors, and visit if it is local.

Investigate. Check with a watchdog group to see how the charity rates (see below).

Examine the organization's finances. Determine how much of your contribution is going directly to the cause as opposed to fundraising and administrative costs. You can ask for materials or check out the charity's financial records online.

Continue to monitor the charity to see that it continues to fulfill its mission. One of the best ways to do this is to volunteer on site.

ONLINE RESOURCES

American Institute of Philanthropy	www.charitywatch.org
BBB Wise Giving Alliance	www.give.org
Charitable Choices	www.charitablechoices.org
Guidestar	www.guidestar.org
Independent Charities of America	www.independentcharities.org

information

☼ Donate your spare change. Buy a cashier's check with it and mail to the charity of your choice.

☼ Match your child's giving. Some families agree to match any contribution their child makes to a charitable cause. For instance, if your daughter donates $5 of her allowance to UNICEF, let her know you will add an additional $5 or $10. This agreement teaches kids by example.

☼ Help start good giving habits early. Most money gurus agree that children learn best when parents teach them to split their allowance into three (not necessarily equal) portions—one for spending, one for saving and one for donating. (Each family can work out the proportions that make the most sense for their children.) This will make the idea of giving and saving a natural part of a child's financial decision-making. It also helps kids begin to realize that everyone—no matter what their income—has something to share. Discuss how the charity money will be donated. Will each child make an individual decision about his or her own money? Or will everyone's money be pooled in a "family fund?"

"The key to charity lies in understanding that it is not just a gift to the receiver, but to the giver as well. The need to be charitable is one of the most fundamental human needs; just as we need food and protection and love, we need to share what has been given to us. If a wealthy person gives arrogantly, thinking that he is doing a great favor, he is sadly mistaken: the favor is being done to him. 'More than the rich man does for the pauper,' say the sages, 'the pauper does for the rich man'."
(Source: www.chabad.org/therebbe/article.asp?AID=60689)

volunteering

☼ Find teachable moments. Teaching children about charity shouldn't be confined to a once-a-month family meeting. If a member of Greenpeace comes to the door, explain to your child why you did or did not contribute. When you're sorting through the mail, discuss the charitable solicitations you receive and how you decide which ones to open and which to toss. Do you give money to people begging on your city's streets? Explain why or why not. These are excellent opportunities to share your values with your children.

Click to Donate

One simple way to donate money—that doesn't cost you a penny—is to visit one-click charity websites. Here's the way it works: Each time you click on the designated button on the site, you automatically donate a certain amount to charity. The money comes from sponsors, whose websites are featured on the page. Pick a few websites of causes that your family supports and have the family member who logs on to the computer spend a few minutes contributing to a cause. (These sites sometimes come and go quickly.) The following are just a few of the possibilities. (For evaluations of one-click sites, go to http://kimberlychapman.com/charitycheck/list.html.)

www.quickdonations.com

www.donationjunction.com

http://clickandsave.8k.com

www.thebreastcancersite.com

www.clearlandmines.com

www.povertyfighters.com

http://rainforest.care2.com

www.solvepoverty.com

www.thehungersite.com

www.therainforestsite.com

Resources for Giving to Charity

Books for Kids

The Giving Box: Create a Tradition of Giving With Your Children by Fred Rogers (Philadelphia: Running Press, 2000). Ages 7 and up. The folktales and fables in this small volume encourage children in the spirit of giving. A "giving box" is also included—a simple way to make donating to charity a family ritual.

Books for Parents

The Giving Family: Raising Our Children to Help Others by Susan Crites Price (Washington, D.C.: Council on Foundations, 2001). Advice on how to nurture charity in children and provide them with the tools to give effectively. Order it from the Council on Foundations; 1828 L Street, NW; Washington, DC 20036; 202-466-6512; www.cof.org.

Robin Hood Was Right: A Guide to Giving Your Money for Social Change by Chuck Collins, Pam Rogers, and Joan P. Garner (New York: W.W. Norton & Co., 2000). Supports the dictum "Change, not charity!" Explains how to give your money to get at the roots of social problems, rather than supporting short-term "band-aid" solutions. Provides guidance for choosing worthwhile causes and strategies for social change.

Organizations and Websites

Independent Sector
www.independentsector.org
202-467-6100
1200 Eighteenth Street, NW, Suite 200, Washington, DC 20036

An organization that works to support not-for-profit and philanthropic work. Check the website for 10 tips for giving wisely, a donor's bill of rights, and tax information related to charitable donations.

Reference

Shollar, L. 2000. *A Thread of Kindness: A Tzedakah Story.* Brooklyn: NY: Hachai Publishing.

Shop With a Conscience

Americans consume a hugely disproportionate share of the world's resources. (For example, the Union of Concerned Scientists reports that we use one-third of the world's paper, despite representing only five percent of the world's population.) By consuming indiscriminately, we are doing real damage to the earth and the world community.

We do have choices, however. Some shampoos, jeans, and breakfast cereals are produced humanely, with social and environmental responsibility in mind. Some companies make an effort to enforce safe and fair working conditions and ethical business standards. And some businesses donate a portion of your dollar to charity. If your family is willing to become educated, you have the power to influence corporate policy. You can spend your money with companies who test products on animals or those that fund projects to protect endangered species. Your dollars can go to businesses that pollute the environment or those that help heal the earth, those that exploit their workers or those that look out for their best interests.

And there's more. If you write to protest socially irresponsible practices, companies listen. The Council on Economic Priorities reports that corporations assume that for every letter of protest they receive, 200 to 500 additional consumers agree with the views of the letter writer and are concerned, as well. The dollars you spend and the opinions you voice as a consumer send critical messages about the kind of world you want to create. Here are some tips for putting your heart into your shopping.

Ideas for Shopping With a Conscience

☼ Use online charitable shopping sites. These organizations give a portion of each sale to a charitable cause.

www.IGive.com	Up to 27% of your purchase goes to your favorite charity.
www.mycause.com	Up to 12% of the purchase price goes to the cause you choose.
www.sc.com	A portion of the revenues are donated to charity.

www.schoolpop.com   A percentage of each purchase goes to the school or youth organization of your choice.

www.workingforchange.com   Up to 5% of every purchase is donated to progressive causes.

☀ Consider the environmental soundness of products and the companies that make them before buying. Here are some questions to ask:

- Is it made from a product that is renewable?

- Is there minimal packaging?

- Do I really need this item?

- Can the packaging be recycled?

- Will it last?

- Is it biodegradable?

- Can I buy it in bulk? (This saves money and packaging.)

☀ Buy energy-saving products and find out how to save energy in your home.

Energy Guide
www.energyguide.com
781-694-3300
16 Laurel Avenue, Suite 100, Wellesley Hills, MA 02481

☀ Learn about the organizations with which you do business.

- Go to www.responsibleshopper.com to help your family make informed decisions about what and where you buy, or consult one of the books in the Resources section below.

- Write letters, e-mail, or telephone companies with whom you do business to ask about their labor practices, charitable giving, investment in the community, environmental record, ethics, and other issues.

- Find out how to research corporations more thoroughly by getting tips from www.corporations.org.

- Check out the records of the garment industry at Sweatshop Watch or the Clean Clothes Campaign.

Sweatshop Watch
www.sweatshopwatch.org
510-834-8990
310 Eighth Street, Suite 303, Oakland, CA 94607

Clean Clothes Campaign
www.cleanclothes.org

- Check Co-op America's Green Pages Online for a directory of socially and environmentally responsible businesses.

Co-op America
www.coopamerica.org
800-58-GREEN
1612 K Street, NW, Suite 600, Washington, DC 20006

Green Pages Online
www.greenpages.org

☼ Support fair trade.

- Shop with retailers who support fair trade. Visit www.fairtradefederation.com to get a list of retailers who ensure their products are made by artisans who are getting a fair price for their labor.

- Buy fair trade products online. (www.globalexchange.org/stores)

- Buy fair trade coffee. For a list of retailers, visit www.globalexchange.org/economy/coffee/retailers.html

- Become a fair trade activist. For information on helping make your city a fair trade zone, visit www.globalexchange.org/ftzone/

- Buy clothing from companies that support fair labor practices. Do your part to end sweatshop conditions both in this country and around the world. Find an online copy of the "Guide to Ending Sweatshops" at www.sweatshops.org.

☼ Take part in online charity auctions.

- Yahoo Charity Auctions, http://help.yahoo.com/help/auct/achar

- e-Bay Charity, http://pages.ebay.com/charity/

- Goodwill, www.shopgoodwill.com

- Missionfish, www.missionfish.com

☼ Boycott companies if their practices are socially irresponsible. Make certain you only take part in a boycott if you're certain of your facts and someone has alerted the company. And be careful not to buy similar products from a company that is just as socially irresponsible. Read Co-op America's "Boycott Action News" for a list of current boycotts and the online "Boycott Organizer's Guide" at www.boycotts.org.

Resources for Shopping With a Conscience

Books for Parents

The Consumer's Guide to Effective Environmental Choices: Practical Advice from the Union of Concerned Scientists by Michael Brower and Warren Leon (New York: Three Rivers Press, 1999). Don't know if using disposable diapers is really harmful to the environment or whether driving a fuel-efficient car is critical to our planet's future? This practical, well-researched, and readable guide lets you know which consumer decisions have the most significant impact on the environment.

Shopping Guide for Caring Consumers 2002: A Guide to Products That Are Not Tested on Animals by People for the Ethical Treatment of Animals (Norfolk, Virginia: PETA, 2001). Use this resource to be sure the products you choose are animal-friendly. There's also a list of health charities that have assured PETA they neither conduct nor fund experiments with animals.

Organizations and Websites

Good Money, Inc.
www.goodmoney.com
207-590-2788
29 Old Orchard Road, Seal Rock Spring #8, Saco, ME 04072
An online resource that links to surveys and articles on socially responsible businesses and investing. Learn about ecotravel, the companies with the best diversity records, and sensible spending and investing.

The Green Money Journal
www.greenmoney.com
505-988-7423
PO Box 67, Santa Fe, NM 87504
For $50 a year, you can subscribe to this journal on spending and investing responsibly. Or visit the website and read past issues.

Infact
www.infact.org
800-688-8797
46 Plympton Street, Boston, MA 02118
A corporate watchdog group famous for its successful Nestle and GE boycotts. The group is currently focusing on the tobacco industry.

National Consumers League

www.nclnet.org

202-835-3323

1701 K Street, NW, Suite 1200, Washington, DC 20006

A list of resources for consumers in the areas of personal finance, health and safety, and the environment. Also, find out about the league's current campaigns, some of which are related to worker fairness.

Social Accountability International

www.cepaa.org

212-684-1414

220 East 23rd Street, Suite 605, New York, NY 10010

This group has devised standards for decent workplace conditions. If you have a complaint or want to see which companies have won the corporate conscience awards, visit the website.

Donate Stuff

Your family may not consider decluttering your home a way to help others, but that outdated computer, too-small sweater, and old eyeglasses can be valuable to people and non-profits in need. Spend a weekend together gathering items you no longer use, box them together, and drive them to their new home. (Some organizations will even pick up the merchandise.) Organize other families in your neighborhood to donate, as well. Make sure all items are in good condition and check to be certain the organization needs the items you're donating. (It involves considerable time and expense for nonprofits to get rid of unsuitable items.) According to the Charities Review Council, if you plan to take a tax deduction for any donated items, it is your responsibility to value the merchandise and keep records of the donation. Feel free to ask the charity for a receipt.

Ideas for Donating Stuff

☼ Donate furniture, clothes, toys, and household goods.

- The Arc: The local chapters are listed online at www.thearc.org or in your phone book under Arc.

- Catholic Charities: Check www.catholiccharitiesusa.org for your local agency.

- The Glass Slipper Project (www.glassslipperproject.org; 312-409-4139): Donate lightly-used prom dresses and accessories to Chicago high school students.

- Goodwill: For your local store, visit www.goodwill.org or look in the white pages.

- Salvation Army: For the location nearest you, check the phone book or visit www.redshield.org.

☼ Donate computers and computer-related stuff.

- Another Byte, Inc., www.recycles.org.

- Floppies for Kiddies, www.usacitylink.com/disks.

- National Cristina Foundation, www.cristina.org.

- Computer Recycling Center, www.crc.org.

- Computers for Schools, www.pcsforschools.org.

- Share the Technology Computer Recycling Project, www.sharetechnology.org.

- World Computer Exchange, www.worldcomputerexchange.org.

☼ Donate your family's unwanted eyeglasses and hearing aids. Or organize a drive to collect them from neighbors, friends, and community members. These items can be reconditioned and used to help those in need.

- LensCrafters/Lion's Club International. Call 800-74-SIGHT for the nearest Lions Eyeglass Recycling Center or drop off the eyeglasses at a local Lions Club or LensCrafters store.

  Lions Club
   www.lionsclubs.org

☼ Donate hair.

- **Wigs for Kids**
  www.wigsforkids.org
  440-333-4433
  Executive Club Building, 21330 Center Ridge Road, Suite C
  Rocky River, OH 44116

- **Locks of Love**
  www.locksoflove.org
  561- 963-1677; 888-896-1588
  2925 10th Avenue North, Suite 102, Lake Worth, FL 33461

☼ Donate pet supplies. Contact the Humane Society of the United States at www.hsus.org.

☼ Donate cell phones.

- CTIA Wireless Foundation, www.wirelessfoundation.org.

- Collective Good, www.collectivegood.com.

☼ Donate used greeting and holiday cards.

St. Jude's Recycled Card Program
www.stjudesranch.org.
St. Jude's Ranch for Children, 100 St. Jude's Street, Boulder City, NV 89005

☼ Donate musical instruments.

● Contact your local school's music program.

● Adopt an Instrument—National Music Donation Program,

www.mustcreate.org/global/global6_1.shtml.

☼ Donate bikes.

● Offer them to neighborhood kids.

● Pedals for Progress, www.p4p.org.

Resources for Donating Stuff

Books for Children

The Berenstain Bears Think of Those in Need by Stan and Jan Berenstain (New York:Random House, 1999). Ages 4-8. Simple story of a family who collects too much stuff and decides to donate it to charity.

Organizations and Websites

Excess Access
www.excessaccess.org
Register and list items on the website that you no longer need and that a nonprofit might want. Check out the special programs for such items as musical instruments and hair. There's also a list of organizations that sell recycled goods.

Just Give
www.justgive.org
This website includes dozens of organizations that are looking for donations.

Appendix

Worksheets and Forms

So, you're excited about the possibilities for family volunteering. Now it's time to choose your project. The worksheets provided here will help guide your family on your journey. (Make copies so you can use them again and again.) First, fill out the Family Volunteering Assessment Survey together. It will aid you in considering the kinds of volunteer projects that might interest all of you and help you respond to questions at potential volunteer sites. Then read through the book and consider your options. Brainstorm some possibilities and list them on the Family Volunteer Project Ideas sheet. Get some information, such as agency addresses and phone numbers (if appropriate), for each project idea. When you've completed a project, whether it's a one-time opportunity or a long-term project, take time to reflect with your family about the experience. Use the Reflections sheet to record your family's responses.

The Appendix also includes appropriate suggestions for kids of all different ages, and volunteerting ideas you can pursue no matter how much or how little time you have. There are ideas for holiday volunteering as well as lists of things your family can do to make less trash and save the planet.

Happy Volunteering!

Family Volunteering Assessment Survey

List your family's skills, personality traits, talents and preferences.

_____

_____

_____

_____

Describe what your family would like to learn from volunteering.

_____

_____

_____

_____

Which causes does your family find most interesting?

_____

_____

_____

_____

List your children's ages.

_____

_____

_____

_____

Describe the best times and locations for your family to volunteer.

_____

_____

_____

_____

List some ideas for volunteer projects your family would consider.

1. _____
2. _____
3. _____
4. _____
5. _____

Family Volunteer Project Ideas

Description of potential volunteer opportunity	Agency and/or volunteer coordinator	Address, phone, website, and email	Requirements (orientation, training, age limits, etc.)	Date(s) and times available	Comments

volunteering

Reflections

Project:

Agency:

Date(s):

Hours Spent:

Family Members Involved:

What We Accomplished:

Reflections:

volunteering

Volunteer Projects for Families With Special Interests

Your family will have the most fun if you choose a project that takes advantages of your interests and talents. Check out these possibilities:

If your family likes the outdoors:
- Help out at a camp for children with disabilities.
- Provide horseback riding experience for children with disabilities.
- Help a farm museum care for its animals.
- Take dogs at an animal shelter for walks.
- Be a frogwatch volunteer.
- Work for the Department of Natural Resources.
- Start a community garden.
- Start a neighborhood waste composting site.
- Work at a national wildlife refuge.
- Clean up litter.
- Adopt-a-highway.
- Adopt a monument.
- Do archaeology.
- Plant trees or flowers for a friend or neighbor who is elderly or disabled.
- Volunteer with the parks department.
- Do yard work for the elderly or disabled.
- Adopt an area of your neighborhood that needs loving care.
- Retrieve trash from local rivers, lakes or streams.
- Grow extra vegetables for the hungry.
- Walk or run to fight disease.
- Start a backyard wildlife habitat project.

If your family wants to work from home:
- Host a foreign student.
- Become a crisis shelter family.
- Join the Box Project.
- Be a foster family for pets awaiting adoption.
- Start a Backyard Wildlife Habitat Project.
- Raise dogs for people with disabilities.
- Become a McGruff House.
- Create a story hour in your neighborhood and read to kids.
- Become an electronic activist.
- Join Amnesty International or Human Rights Watch.
- Write letters to the editor or to government officials or write an article about an issue that concerns your family.
- Invite someone who is alone to a meal, especially at holiday time.
- Join the Peter Pan Birthday Club.
- Raise a monkey as an aide to a person with a disability.
- Conduct a letter-writing campaign on environmental issues.

- Sew, knit, or crochet for the needy.
- Sponsor a child overseas.
- Become an e-mail pen pal with a resident of a nursing home or an individual with mental retardation.
- Help produce talking books for the blind, dyslexic and physically disabled.
- Care for a foster child.

If your family wants to combine community service with donating to charity:
- Join the Box Project.
- Sponsor a child overseas.
- Join Feed the Children.
- Sponsor an animal.
- Join Amnesty International or Human Rights Watch.
- Adopt a family or a child for gift-giving at holiday time.
- Organize a fundraiser.
- Take part in a toy drive.
- Fill stockings to donate.
- Collect money for UNICEF at Halloween.
- Donate supplies to an animal shelter.
- Donate items to a homeless shelter.
- Donate books to those in need.
- Collect and donate shoes and socks to orphanages.

If your family likes sports:
- Volunteer to help with Special Olympics.
- Assist coaches for school sports.
- Get involved with America Scores.

If your family is handy:
- Repair old bikes.
- Adopt a room at a shelter.
- Help repair and revitalize homes.
- Help build houses.
- Install deadbolt locks, chain locks and peepholes for elderly residents.
- Help with shelter maintenance.

If your family enjoys driving:
- Drive elderly people to medical appointments or the grocery store.
- Take nursing home residents or isolated seniors to visit their friends or drive friends to visit them.
- Help people with AIDS or cancer get to medical appointments or support groups, or run errands.
- Deliver food from a food pantry to the homebound.
- Deliver meals.
- Provide transportation for pets needing rescue or awaiting adoption.

- Volunteer to drive animals to and from veterinary hospitals to be spayed or neutered.
- Deliver a holiday meal turkey or holiday basket to someone in need.
- Drive seniors to holiday parties.
- Make deliveries to nursing home residents or elderly neighbors.

If your family is artistic:
- Make greeting cards.
- Sew, knit, or crochet for the needy.
- Teach arts and crafts at a community center or after-school program.
- Offer to do face painting or body art for children.
- Photograph kids for a school newsletter.
- Volunteer at an arts and crafts fair.
- Paint a mural.
- Decorate your neighborhood for the holidays.
- Decorate a shelter or nursing home for the holidays.
- Help wrap holiday gifts.
- Help an older neighbor or friend decorate for the holidays.
- Make Christmas stockings. Then fill them and donate them.
- Buy and decorate reusable shopping bags for family and friends.
- Conduct a craft activity at a pediatric ward of a local hospital or a nearby children's hospital.

If your family is musical:
- Perform at a school, nursing home, or senior center.
- Teach an instrument at an after-school class.
- Provide holiday entertainment at a nursing home, senior center, or shelter.
- Be part of a caroling group.
- Start a community band or orchestra.

If your family wants to learn about other cultures:
- Host a foreign student.
- Help refugee families.
- Take a volunteer vacation overseas.
- Publish a multi-cultural newsletter, or start an International Fair at your neighborhood school.

If your family wants to commit random acts of kindness:
- Invite an elderly person to your home for a meal.
- Make a meal for a family whose loved one is sick or in the hospital.
- Provide free babysitting to a struggling family in your neighborhood.
- Offer to walk a dog or provide other care for the pet of a neighbor who is elderly or disabled.
- Welcome a new neighbor.
- Rake, mow, shovel snow, or garden for a neighbor or elderly friend.

Easy, Same-Day, No-Planning Family Volunteer Projects

One Saturday morning you and your kids wake up, eat breakfast, and decide you want to spend some time making a contribution. You haven't talked to a volunteer center, contacted a non-profit agency, or set up an appointment with the volunteer coordinator of the local homeless shelter or crisis nursery. In fact, you've made no plans at all. Not to worry. Your family can still spend the entire day, or any part of it, volunteering. Here are some spur-of-the-moment ideas to consider. (For other last-minute project ideas, visit www.familycares.org.)

If you have 30 minutes, your family can:
- Send out an e-mail in response to an action alert from an organization you support.
- Donate unwanted eyeglasses or hearing aids.
- Sponsor a child overseas.
- Join Feed the Children.
- Sponsor an animal.
- Join Amnesty International.
- Clean up your side of the block.
- Welcome a new neighbor.
- Plant some trees or flowers.
- Call or write elected officials.
- Write a letter to the editor of your local newspaper.
- Write a letter or make a call to a company that uses animals for cosmetic testing and let them know you will boycott their products.
- Offer to walk dogs or provide other pet care for friends or neighbors who are elderly or disabled.
- Sign up for a walk or run to fight disease.
- Give to one of the free charity sites online.
- Send an e-mail to an elderly person or an individual with intellectual disabilities.

If you have two hours, your family can:
- Make a meal for a family whose loved one is sick or in the hospital.
- Provide free babysitting to a struggling family in your neighborhood.
- Donate food to a food bank.
- Collect your own toys for children in a family shelter.
- Create a list of shelters and soup kitchens to give to those in need.
- Create a neighborhood map or directory.
- Buy and decorate reusable shopping bags for family and friends.
- Donate books to people who need them.
- Visit with residents of a nursing home.
- Donate supplies to an animal shelter.
- Invite an isolated elderly person to your home for a meal.

- ☼ Buy and plant a tree.
- ☼ Clean up litter.

If you have one-half day, your family can:
- ☼ Invite an elderly person to your home for a meal.
- ☼ Collect donations from neighbors and friends, such as:
  - Food for a food bank
  - Books for a hospital or shelter
  - Hats for the American Cancer Society
  - Toys for kids at a homeless shelter
  - Mittens and hats to a homeless shelter or crisis nursery
  - Supplies to an animal shelter
- ☼ Bake cookies or another special treat for residents of a homeless shelter.
- ☼ Research and write articles or letters to your local newspaper editor to raise awareness of endangered species or another environmental issue.
- ☼ Repair an old bike and donate it to a child in need.
- ☼ Tape children's books and take them to kids in the hospital.
- ☼ Plant trees or flowers for a neighbor or friend who is elderly or disabled.
- ☼ Make greeting cards and deliver them to a hospital or nursing home.
- ☼ Put together health, baby, or school kits for Church World Service.
- ☼ Become informed about an issue on which your family may want to take action.

If you have one full day, your family can:
- ☼ Knit, crochet, quilt, bake or put together activity boxes.
- ☼ Attend a local cultural event and then write a review for a neighborhood newspaper.
- ☼ Create and distribute material on safety to your neighbors.
- ☼ Aid a homebound elderly person with laundry, yard work, or house cleaning.
- ☼ Start a Backyard Wildlife Habitat Project.
- ☼ Start a neighborhood waste composting site.
- ☼ Begin planning a fundraiser.
- ☼ Begin organizing a partnership between your faith community and another church, temple, or synagogue.

Developmental Timetable for Child Volunteers

As you're contemplating your volunteer work, you may wonder just how much you can expect and ask from your little ones. To help you, here are a few basics to remember about child development. The characteristics provided for each age group are, of course, generalizations and may not apply to any individual child. Use this table as a general guide, making allowances for your own child's temperament and rate of development. In addition, the recommended volunteer projects can sometimes be suitable for a younger child, depending on his or her personality, development, and the circumstances of the situation. (For example, it may be appropriate to cook a meal at a homeless shelter with an infant if there is an additional adult available to take care of the child.) In all cases, the opportunities recommended for younger children are perfectly suitable for older children as well.

INFANTS AND TODDLERS

Characteristics of Infants:
- Cry when they hear others cry
- Can be carried along easily
- Bring joy when seen and held by others
- Begin to experience stranger fear and separation anxiety at about eight months

Characteristics of Toddlers:
- Will listen to stories with pictures
- Engage in simple conversation
- Have difficulty controlling impulses
- Find it hard to share
- Have minimal desire to please others
- Demonstrate caring acts, such as putting dolls to bed
- Like to offer comfort, though response may not always be appropriate
- Routine is important

Possible Volunteer Projects:
- Walk or run to fight disease.
- Adopt a grandparent.
- Visit with nursing home residents.
- Take part in peaceful rallies or demonstrations.
- Get involved in any in-home projects. (See Volunteer Projects for Families With Special Interests, page 179.)
- Drive or make deliveries. (See Volunteer Projects for Families With Special Interests, page 179.)
- Include a person with a disability on family outings.
- Form a friendship with an individual with mental retardation.

PRESCHOOLERS

Characteristics:

- Show sympathy and compassion to others
- Like to play with peers, especially by age 4
- May begin to notice differences between people and make embarrassing comments
- Often are social and talkative
- Use imaginative play and like to dress up
- Show more interest in family activities
- Show compassion when it doesn't conflict with own desires
- Respond more appropriately to empathy than when younger
- Like to do chores and be helpful
- Remain strongly attached to parents
- Can begin to empathize with those they've never met through stories, movies, or television

Possible Volunteer Projects:

- Read your family's favorite books to children in the hospital or in the waiting room of a hospital or clinic.
- Assemble comfort kits for the Red Cross, kits for Church World Service, or activity boxes for needy children.
- Work at a food bank.
- Donate hats to the American Cancer Society.
- Collect and donate children's books to a hospital's pediatric ward.

SCHOOL-AGE KIDS

Characteristics:

- Being helpful is looked on positively by peers
- Like art projects
- Like dramatization
- Can help with household and yard tasks
- May be tense in new situations
- Want to be considered important by adults
- Consider family activities to be important
- Begin to empathize with groups of afflicted people (homeless, victims of natural disasters, etc.)
- Are concerned about people's conditions (poverty, illness, etc.), rather than just their momentary emotions
- Display budding interest in social and political issues
- Moral reasoning can be advanced by discussing issues of ethics
- Are increasingly cooperative
- Can use the telephone
- Can help solve problems
- Are increasingly able to adopt another's point of view
- Generally have an industrious approach to productive work
- Display greater ability to appreciate the perspective of others

Possible Volunteer Projects:

- Pick up litter.
- Plan and carry out a craft night or organize a party at a nursing home.
- Bring your family pet along to a nursing home.
- Make deliveries of gifts, food, flowers, or books to nursing home residents, elderly neighbors, or hospital patients.
- Visit children in the hospital. Put on a puppet show or conduct a craft activity.
- Socialize with a special needs child.
- Work on school fundraising events.
- Buy and decorate reusable shopping bags for family and friends.
- Perform a family talent show at a nursing home.
- Mentor an at-risk family or child, or befriend a family whose child is in the hospital.
- Take dinner to a family in need.
- Cook at a soup kitchen or homeless shelter.
- Volunteer to glean.
- Help an elderly person with laundry, yard work, and house cleaning.
- Send mail to sick children.

PRETEENS

Characteristics:

- May be inhibited by peer pressure and how peers judge them
- Can consider more abstract issues and questions
- More interested in peer activities than family activities
- Need independence
- Interested in money-making
- Need recognition
- Increasingly value relationships with others

Possible Volunteer Projects:

- Work with younger children in a hospital, at a daycare center, or at a camp.
- Become an e-mail pen pal with a nursing home resident or person with mental retardation.
- Provide free babysitting to a struggling family in your neighborhood.
- Organize a fundraiser.
- Take homeless children on field trips.
- Work at a children's museum.
- Start a Care Bags for Kids program.
- Initiate or help with activities at a nursing home or senior center.
- Help out in the pediatric ward of a local hospital or in a children's hospital.
- Help at a Ronald McDonald House.
- Befriend a chronically ill child in his or her home.
- Form a special relationship with a person with AIDS.
- Tape children's books and take them to kids in the hospital.

- Assist in a group home for the disabled.
- Socialize with a special-needs child.

TEENS

Characteristics:
- Enjoy working with peers
- Need significant projects
- Begin to think about career paths
- Begin to understand abstract ideas about justice, law, politics, and government
- Have a more developed sense of social justice
- Make moral judgments on their own values rather than based on social convention or persuasion of authority
- Are remaking relationship with family and moving into autonomy while maintaining strong emotional attachments
- Desire freedom but sensitive to parental influence
- Display more complex thinking about social issues
- Helping others and instruction in moral issues advances moral thinking

Possible Volunteer Projects:
- Hold and rock babies.
- Help build, repair, and revitalize homes.
- Provide horseback riding experience for children with disabilities.
- Work for a candidate your family supports.
- Get involved in a cause.
- Tutor or read to children.
- Help elderly people write their life story to pass down to their grandchildren and great grandchildren.
- Play with kids after school.
- Get out the vote.
- Become a blood donor or help with a blood drive.
- Organize first aid training for a school or community group.
- Volunteer at a zoo or aquarium.

"Ways to 'Live Green'" Refrigerator Reminders

Copy the following pages and post them on your refrigerator to remind your family of the importance of "living green."

If You Want to Save the Planet...

Your family can heal the planet with the lifestyle decisions you make each day. Here are some simple ways your family can "go green."

If you want to save energy and reduce global warming, you can:

- Keep your heat low in the winter and reduce air conditioning consumption in the summer. (Put on or take off that sweater instead.)
- Buy compact fluorescent light bulbs (www.energystar.gov/products/cfls/).
- Dry clothes on a clothesline instead of in the dryer.
- Close the refrigerator door quickly.
- Insulate your home.
- Fix faucet leaks.
- Turn off lights.
- Plant trees to absorb carbon dioxide.
- Walk or bike instead of using your car.

If you want to protect animals and habitats, you can:

- Buy "dolphin-safe" tuna.
- Don't buy the following items: Ivory, teak, mahogany, feathers, tortoise shells, fur, coral or bone jewelry.
- Don't bother or destroy wild animals and plants.
- Don't release helium balloons. Some sea animals choke on them when they fall back to earth.
- Don't buy products tested on animals.

If you want to reduce pollution, you can:

- Use bikes, feet, or public transportation instead of your car.
- Don't use pesticides or chemicals on your lawn or in your garden.
- Don't litter.
- Use less energy (see above).
- Eat organic food. Farmers raising organic food don't use chemicals that can pollute the environment.
- Dispose of hazardous waste (such as car oil) carefully and correctly.

© Robins Lane Press 800.638.0928 www.robinslane.com
Publisher permits photocopying of this page for distribution.

20 Ways to Make Less Trash

Americans produce more garbage than any people in the world. If your family wants to do its part to limit trash production, focus on reducing, reusing and recycling. Here are some specific ways you can reduce your own mountain of trash.

1. Take your name off catalog mailing lists. Register online at www.dmaconsumers.org or send your full name, home address, and signature to: DMA Mail Preference Service

   P.O. Box 643, Carmel, NY 10512
2. Use both sides of a piece of paper. Then recycle it.
3. Wrap gifts in newspaper, old maps, magazine pages, or tissue from gift boxes.
4. Use recycled products and recycle the products you use.
5. Start a compost heap.
6. Use cloth grocery bags or reuse your paper and plastic ones.
7. Buy items in bulk instead of those packaged separately. And buy items with less packaging. (One-third of all garbage is packaging.)
8. Buy used when possible.
9. Make your own greeting cards with recycled paper.
10. Use sponges, rags, or a cloth towel instead of paper towels.
11. Use rechargeable batteries.
12. Use compact fluorescent light bulbs.
13. Use bars of soap instead of pump bottles.
14. Wash and reuse aluminum foil. Recycle it when done.
15. Give extra wire coat hangers to a dry cleaning business.
16. Don't eat fast food. There's too much packaging. When ordering take out, decline the plastic utensils and instead use your own (reusable) flatware.
17. Donate stuff that's still usable instead of throwing it away.
18. Use reusable lunch bags or boxes rather than paper.
19. Buy any items you can in returnable containers.
20. Encourage your school, park, church, or local business to stop using unrecyclable plastic and Styrofoam for packing and storing. Approach the situation with respect and care.

Holiday Volunteering Ideas

While the stresses and commitments of the holidays often keep families from enjoying one another, volunteer work can be an oasis of time you and your family can spend together. Service work can counter the commercialism and consumerism that has come to dominate so many of the holidays. And because these volunteer opportunities are often one-time or limited duration, they can be used to discover if the volunteer job or agency is the right one for your family. But get started early. Some organizations can be inundated with volunteers, particularly around Thanksgiving and Christmas.

Martin Luther King Jr. Day

Take part in a celebration or parade. Many communities organize events for the day. Volunteer to help out or organize your own if nothing is planned.

Give a presentation honoring Dr. King to your school or in the community. For background, check your local library or visit one of the many websites honoring his life and work.

Work to have your community or city officially recognize the holiday. While Martin Luther King, Jr. Day is a national holiday, some cities don't recognize it. If yours is one of them, work to change that.

Send free e-mail cards reminding others of Dr. King's life and dreams. Visit www.holidays.net/mlk to find out how.

Choose any one-day service project. Look through this book and pick out one project your family can tackle for the day. Start a tradition of service to celebrate Dr. King's birthday.

Valentine's Day

Make and deliver Valentine's cards to a veteran's hospital, nursing home, or hospital. Gather construction paper, paper doilies, ribbon, markers and glitter to produce fabulous homemade cards. Then deliver them to hospital patients. Take some time to visit. Or make heart-shaped candy holders: cut two identical hearts from construction paper, decorate, and then glue them together, leaving the top open. Stuff with Valentine candy and deliver to children at a homeless shelter or hospital.

Throw a Valentine's party for the children at a homeless shelter or residents of a nursing home. Offer some heart-shaped cookies or cake and red punch, decide on a Valentine's craft, and include some entertainment or games.

Act as "sweethearts" to seniors by delivering flowers, chocolates, and visits. Some area Little Brothers-Friends of the Elderly (www.littlebrothers.org) sponsor this event. If the one in your area doesn't, organize it yourselves.

Easter

Distribute Easter baskets. Either volunteer to deliver baskets put together by a local social service organization or "build" your own. Consider including food, personal hygiene items (toothbrush, shampoo), or small toys and candy for children.

Sponsor an Easter egg hunt. Hide eggs for kids to find. Organize children from your neighborhood, a homeless shelter, a Head Start program, or community center.

Dress up as Easter bunnies and deliver eggs. Stuff plastic eggs with candy, don your bunny costumes, and distribute them to children at a shelter, hospital, or orphanage.

Assist kids with Easter craft projects. Dying eggs is often a child's fondest memory of the season. Create that memory for children in a shelter or hospital.

Deliver an Easter meal to a homebound person. With Meals on Wheels programs often closed on holidays, your family can step in when a hot meal and companionship are most needed.

Serve an Easter meal. Set up, cook, serve and clean up an Easter meal at a homeless shelter or soup kitchen. For an extra treat, bring along spring flowers to place on the tables.

Halloween

Collect money for UNICEF. To find out where to get the collection boxes (or to download them), how to donate money, and what your donation is used for, visit www.unicefusa.org/trickortreat or contact U.S. Fund for UNICEF, 800-FOR-KIDS.

Collect food while trick-or-treating. Or have a Halloween party and ask your guests to bring canned food. Donate it to a local food shelf.

Host or volunteer at a Halloween party for a homeless shelter, hospital, or nursing home. Decorate, help with games or crafts, or serve refreshments.

Coordinate a community Halloween party as an alternative to trick or treating. If you think it's safer for children to avoid the door-to-door Halloween tradition, host a party at a neighborhood center for the kids.

Wear costumes and pass out candy at a shelter or children's home. You and your children can get creative by dressing up to delight the kids.

Collect new (or used) costumes. Or make Halloween costumes for low-income children. Donate to a school, shelter or children's service organization.

Collect old eyeglasses while trick or treating. Some local Lion's Clubs (partnering with LensCrafters) sponsor a "Sight Night" when people collect used eyewear for recycling. You can also pass out brochures that list community drop-off boxes for later donations (www.lionsclubs.org).

Read Halloween stories to kids at your local library. Some good picks include *The Hallo-Weiner* by Dav Pilkey (New York: Scholastic, Inc., 1999) and *Georgie* by Robert Bright (New York: Farrar, Straus and Giroux, 1999).

Volunteer at a Halloween attraction. Zoos, farms, and other venues are often looking for volunteers to dress up and entertain families for special Halloween events.

Thanksgiving, Christmas, Hanukkah and Kwanzaa

Deliver holiday meals. Often, Meals on Wheels programs do not have regular service on Thanksgiving or Christmas. Volunteers can help out by delivering a meal to the homebound. Spend some time talking and sharing. Your family may be the person's only holiday visitor.

Deliver a basket with everything a family needs for a holiday meal. Include turkey, potatoes, cranberry sauce, bread, vegetables, and pies or whatever the traditional holiday foods might be. You can also add table decorations and other practical items a family might enjoy. Call the Salvation Army, America's Second Harvest or your local food bank to find out if a local organization is sponsoring this effort.

Take part in a toy drive. Volunteers are needed for pick up and delivery, sorting, wrapping, registering families, and handing out gifts. Call your local Salvation Army or volunteer center. Or visit www.toysfortots.org.

Help wrap holiday gifts. Department stores sometimes have opportunities for volunteers to wrap, with the proceeds benefiting charity. Or, organizations receiving toy donations may need wrappers.

Offer to take an elderly person shopping. Some people may not be able to shop for holiday gifts without assistance. Your family can provide both transportation and help with gift buying and wrapping.

Help out at a shelter, nursing home, children's home, hospital or a residence for the developmentally disabled.

- **Decorate for the holidays.** Create a festive atmosphere by decorating tables for a Thanksgiving meal (autumn-colored candles, cornucopia centerpiece, mini pumpkins, and squash) and the lobbies or dining halls with fall colors (burnt orange, dark greens, and reds). For Christmas, consider decorating tables with red and green candles, surrounded by a pine garland. For Hanukkah, you might use blue and white flowers, menorahs, and dreidels. Kwanzaa decorations often include African motifs.

- **Pretend to be Santa and his elves.** Nothing is more delightful to children than being visited by Santa and his helpers.

- **Host or help out at a holiday party.** This might include decorating, buying, and serving refreshments or organizing entertainment.

- **Give music.** Be part of a caroling group. Or play a piano in the lobby.

- **Give a performance.** Put on a holiday puppet show or talent show or lead a holiday sing-a-long.

- **Donate decorations such as Christmas trees, ornaments, lights, or menorahs.** These can be used year after year.

- **Visit.** Make this a special time for children and adults who can't be at home or with loved ones during the holidays. Adults may just appreciate some conversation, a holiday card or gift. Children would love a small stocking or having their picture taken with a Polaroid camera. (See Chapter 3 for visiting ideas.)

Help an older neighbor or friend decorate. Volunteer to help someone who may not have the resources or ability to decorate their home or apartment for the holidays. Call senior services in your area to be matched with an individual who might appreciate help.

Fill stockings to donate. For adults in nursing homes or shelters, the stocking could contain sample-size hygiene and cosmetic products, cards, and books. For children in hospitals or shelters, include small toys, puzzle books, stuffed animals, crayons, and candy.

Adopt a family or a child for gift-giving. This is a great holiday project that will get your child's mind off the "gimmes" for a while. Find an organization that matches your family with a low-income family and provides a list of gifts the family has asked for. Your family does the shopping and wrapping. Call the Salvation Army or your local volunteer center.

Ring bells for the Salvation Army. This is the organization's largest fundraising effort. Your family can staff a kettle for as many hours as you wish. Contact the Salvation Army nearest you.

Drive seniors to holiday parties. Help older people living at home or in nursing homes get out and about this season. Call senior services in your area or a volunteer center to ask about becoming a holiday driver.

Make and deliver holiday cards or gifts. These could go to children, seniors, or others who might need a thoughtful gesture during the holidays.

Cook and/or serve a holiday meal at a homeless shelter or soup kitchen. Help with a holiday dinner by cooking, serving, and cleaning up.

Make ornaments and holiday decorations. Donate them to low-income families or institutions to brighten someone's holidays.

Be a surrogate family to an individual in an institution. Include someone in your holidays who might otherwise be alone. Take the person to dinner, to a special event, or bring him or her to your home.

Spend part of the holiday with a person who's homebound. Perhaps you know a neighbor or family member who could use company. If not, contact senior services in your area to find out if there's someone who would enjoy your family's visit.

Index

Organization Index